A decade of change in free-access higher education

Richard I. Ferrin   *19-40*

College Entrance Examination Board, New York, 1971

Copies of this book may be ordered from Publications Order Office, College Entrance Examination Board, Box 592, Princeton, New Jersey 08540. The price is $1.50.
   Editorial inquiries concerning this book should be addressed to Editorial Office, College Entrance Examination Board, 888 Seventh Avenue, New York, New York 10019.

Library of Congress Catalog Card Number: 71-171378

Printed in the United States of America

Contents

Preface

The United States has invested considerable resources — both financial and otherwise — in expanding access to higher education over the past decade, and this study attempts to provide one index of the success of that investment. This report is a condensation and revision of a doctoral dissertation completed while I was both a student at Stanford University and on the staff of the College Board's Access Research Office in Palo Alto, California.

Warren Willingham, Director of the Access Research Office, recently conducted a national study of the accessibility of higher education. Published as *Free-Access Higher Education,* the study included an analysis of the populations living near an inexpensive, nonselective college in various geographic areas in 1968. By employing a similar quantitative approach to educational accessibility, by gathering similar data for 1958, and by comparing the two sets of data, this present study sought to indicate the extent to which this type of educational opportunity has changed over the past decade.

Chapter 1 lays the background for the study and briefly discusses the financial, academic, motivational, and geographic barriers that continue to limit access to higher education for so many young people. Chapter 2 describes both the shift toward inaccessibility by established institutions and the growth of new accessible colleges. Chapter 3 analyzes the effects such changes have had upon the populations in various geographic areas. Chapter 4 isolates several factors that have affected institutional accessibility and analyzes the impact of each factor over the past decade. Chapter 5 summarizes the key developments of the 1960s and suggests possible implications of these developments for the 1970s.

When one embarks upon a project such as this, he tends to do so with his head in the clouds but his feet in the sand. The assistance of numerous people is required both to bring him down to earth and to get him moving along a reasonable and profitable path. Such was very much the case with this study. Many people deserve credit for their efforts on my behalf. Among them were the members of my dissertation committee, Lewis Mayhew, Victor Baldridge, and Dudley Kirk, who each offered encouragement, support, and constructive criticism, with each type of response coming when and where it was most appropriate.

Warren Willingham has been a constant source of support and ideas from the conception of this study to its emergence as a completed document. While he contributed much to the strengths of this report, I alone am responsible for its shortcomings and inaccuracies.

Becky Daniels, Heidi Facer, and Judith Gray have also earned my sincere gratitude for their capable gathering and analyzing of the large amount of data necessitated by the objectives of this study. In addition, Judith's editorial and secretarial skill was not only a valuable resource but also a joy to behold, and Heidi's typing of the manuscript was painstakingly and expertly carried out.

Ann Kaufman and Diane Olsen of the College Board publications staff have used their special skills to translate the manuscript into a publishable report.

Only now do I fully realize why most men conclude a preface with a simple but obviously heartfelt expression of appreciation to their wives. For what can you say in this short space to a woman who has understood your preoccupation, blended gentle prodding with unrestrained love, been both a devoted mother and father to your children, and endured an abnormal life style and time schedule? You can really only say "thanks for putting up with it and standing with me through it all," and it is exactly that which I want to communicate to my wife Margie at this time and through this medium.

1. The nature of accessible higher education

Since its formal establishment in 1636, higher education in the United States has assumed a multitude of purposes. It has been asked to educate for citizenship, for world and intercultural understanding, for self-understanding, for freedom, for vocation, for equality of opportunity, and, more recently, for opportunity for equality. The problem would not be so great if one purpose superseded the other, but such has not been the case. In 1970 institutions are generally expected to accomplish all, or certainly most, of the above purposes as well as a great number that have not been listed. The task is staggering.

Despite the realization that any discussion focused on a single purpose is, at best, of limited utility to educational administrators and planners, and despite agreement with the holistic view of higher education as expressed by the statement, "an educational institution is like a snake; touch it at any spot and it wriggles all over," this report deals primarily with the single issue of equality of opportunity. More specifically, it is concerned with one facet of that issue; that is, the extent to which institutions of higher learning have been made accessible to various populations over the past decade. This investigation was made possible by the availability of data from a national demographic analysis of those people who lived within commuting distance of an inexpensive, nonselective institution as of fall 1968 (Willingham, 1970). In this study similar data were developed for 1958, and the two sets of data were examined to determine what changes had occurred between 1958 and 1968 and what factors were instrumental in effecting these changes. For example, what demographic effect has the great influx of new community colleges had on

Table 1. Indices of expansion of higher education
1948, 1958, and 1968

Year	Number of institutions	Total enrollment	Current-fund expenditures (billions of 1968-69 dollars)[g]
1948-49	1,808[a]	2,500,000[d]	2.8[e]
1958-59	1,903[b] (+ 5%)	3,442,556[b] (+ 38%)	6.0[e] (+114%)
1968-69	2,491[c] (+31%)	7,571,636[c] (+120%)	19.0[f] (+217%)
Percent change 1948-68	+38	+203	+579

a. Willingham, p. 4.
b. *1958 Opening Fall Enrollment, Analytic Report,* pp. 2-3.
c. *1968 Opening Fall Enrollment, Part A,* pp. 3-5.
d. *Digest of Educational Statistics,* 1968, p. 68.
e. Estimated from *Higher Education Finances,* 1968, p. 3.
f. Projected from *College and University Bulletin,* December 1, 1969, p. 5.
g. .80 1968-69 dollars = .99 1958-59 dollars = 1.20 1948-49 dollars, according to *Statistical Abstract of the United States, 1969,* Table 500, p. 339.

the accessibility of higher education? And, how many institutions have become so selective within the past 10 years that they are no longer accessible to a large segment of the population?

Higher education in the United States has expanded in many directions since the end of World War II and since the 1947 publication of that often-referred-to "accessibility document," the Truman Report (*Higher Education for American Democracy,* 1947). Money has poured in, new institutions have cropped up, existing institutions have increased both their facilities and their personnel, those responsible for state planning and central coordination have tried to bring order to what has been, at times, Topsy-like institutional development, and above all, enrollments have increased at a phenomenal and somewhat unexpected rate. The major portion of this increase has occurred since the late 1950s (Table 1), being spurred by the news of Sputnik and the resulting National Defense Education Act.

Also in the late 1950s many state leaders realized that the educational needs of a large portion of their citizens were not being met. Recognizing that democratization of higher education was not likely to come from the private sector and only to a small degree from the existing public four-year colleges and universities, they finally began to adopt a key recommendation of the Truman Report and make provisions for public, low-cost, nonselective, easily accessible two-year institutions. For example, in 1957 alone, 18 states passed legislation leading either to the establishment or expansion of such institutions (Blocker, Plummer, and Richardson, 1965). Public two-year colleges, which had increased from 257 to only 290 in the decade 1948-1958, were built at a rate of more than one every two weeks in the decade 1958-1968 (*Digest of Educational Statistics,* 1968). In fact by 1968, 595 of these institutions were in operation with many more at various stages of development.

Enrollment at public two-year colleges also increased at remarkable rates both in absolute terms and in comparison with the rapid rise in enrollment for higher education in general. Whereas the degree-credit enrollment for all institutions increased 34 percent in the decade 1948-1958 and 109 percent between 1958 and 1968, the degree-credit enrollment for public two-year colleges grew 115 percent and 254 percent, respectively. (Figure A.) During this same period the proportion of all degree-credit students in higher education who were attending public two-year colleges increased from 6 percent in 1948 to 10 percent in 1958 and to 17 percent in 1968. (Figure B.) Not included in these figures are the more than a half million nondegree-credit students who enrolled in two-year institutions in 1968 (United States Office of Education, 1969), a group more than three times as large as the group that attended all higher institutions a decade earlier (United States Office of Education, 1966).

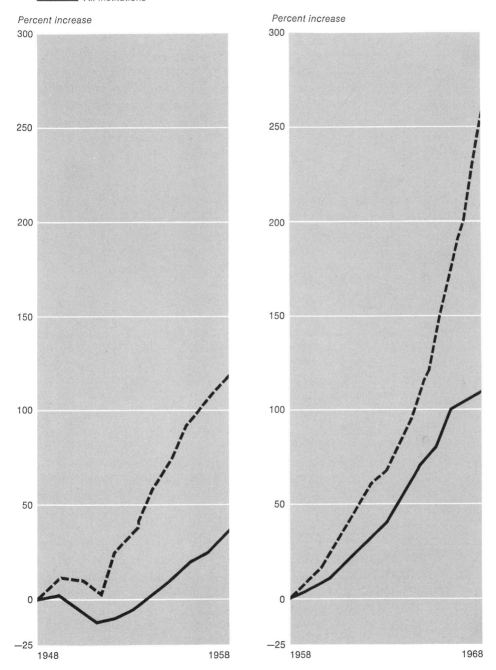

Figure A. Change in percentage of degree-credit enrollment
for all institutions and for public two-year colleges, 1948, 1958, and 1968

Enrollment (millions)

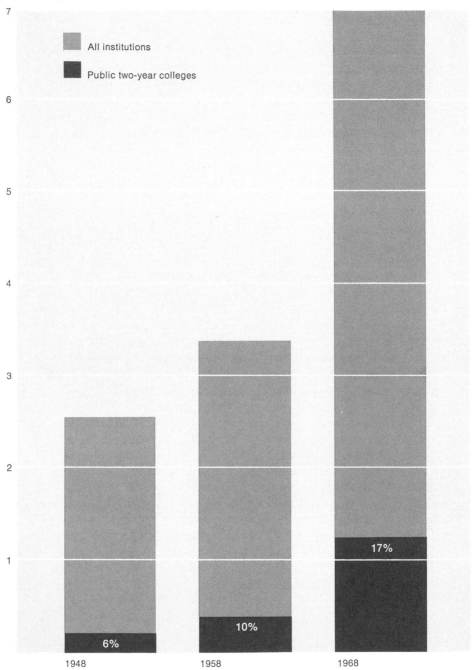

Figure B. Numerical growth in degree-credit enrollment for all institutions and for public two-year colleges, 1948, 1958, and 1968

Barriers to universal higher education[1]

While there can be no doubt that the day of mass higher education has arrived, at the same time there can be no doubt that the day of universal opportunity for higher education has not. Despite the fact that college enrollments and expenditures have increased dramatically and new institutions have been and are being established in heretofore collegeless communities, far more young people could profit from further education than are now attending college (Knoell, 1966). Gross inequities in college attendance still exist among various categories of young people, with the low-income, nonwhite individual bearing the brunt of this unequal distribution of educational resources. For example, in a 1969 study of enrollments at 80 of the most prominent state universities in the United States, black students, on the average, represented only 2 percent of the student population.

In no institution was the proportion of blacks as high as 12 percent (the figure for the proportion of blacks in the national population) (Egerton, 1969).

In Coleman's 1965-66 survey of enrollments at more than 2,000 institutions, he found that only 20 public and 26 private institutions had between 10 and 50 percent blacks. In other words, most black students attending college either went to a predominantly black institution, typically located in the South, or to an institution where there were fewer than 10 percent blacks. Nearly two-thirds of this latter group of colleges enrolled fewer than 2 percent blacks (Coleman, 1966).

A third survey, this one conducted by the American Council on Education, gives further evidence that blacks in particular and students from low-income families in general are still underrepresented among college attendees. The results of questionnaires administered to students entering college in fall 1969 showed that only 6 percent reported themselves to be blacks and only 28 percent reported that they came from families earning less than $8,000 in 1968.

Politicians and college administrators have become quite aware of the educational inequities that continue to plague this country, but they often speak optimistically of the programs that have come into being and the great strides that are being taken. Ghetto workers, on the other hand, are often more cynical in their appraisal of the current scene. The comment made by one such individual is indicative of the reactions of many: "When the year's verbiage about ghetto youths' greater educational opportunity is matched against the actual increase of ghetto youth in today's college classrooms, the gap can embarrass any dean of admissions" (Selk, 1969).

As one seriously ponders this statement and the lack of educational opportunity that most certainly still remains among groups of individuals, he is compelled to go the next step and ask: Why this gap? What barriers have limited

1. The author undertook a more thorough treatment of this topic, including an examination of several barriers and a presentation of efforts taken throughout the nation in the past decade to reduce them, in an unpublished monograph, "Barriers to Universal Higher Education," Palo Alto, California, College Entrance Examination Board, 1970.

access to higher education for certain individuals? What obstacles stand in the way of further, more rapid expansion of higher educational opportunities?

Many researchers have studied this problem over the past 20 years and through their investigations have identified and examined several obstacles that tend to restrict access. In general, the barriers identified appear to fall into four basic categories—finances, academics, motivation, and geography.

With respect to these barriers, it would be well worth remembering that "The nature of a hindrance to college attendance depends more on the potential student's perception of the difficulty, in many respects, than it does on the true character of the problem" (Martyn, 1966). In other words, if any one or more of these four categories is perceived as a barrier, then, in fact, it does become one for that particular individual.

Many efforts to eliminate or even reduce the conditions restricting certain individuals from taking advantage of higher education have tended wisely to attack multiple barriers simultaneously. Architects of these proposals have recognized that to concentrate on only one would certainly be ineffective if the other three continue to restrict accessibility. In recent years state master planners have recommended most frequently "the creation of new junior colleges, expansion of existing four-year institutions, and creation of new institutions in populated areas where no public institution exists" (Mayhew, 1969).

Junior colleges particularly have attempted to attack the financial barrier by charging little or no tuition, the academic barrier by having "open-door" admissions policies, and the geographic barrier by locating in densely populated areas. Since the motivational barrier typically develops in the elementary and secondary school years, these colleges are left with the task of finding ways to "turn on" those who have been "turned off" by education in the past. The mere presence of a low-cost, open-door institution within the community may influence some marginal students to attend, but it is likely to have a more substantial impact if it is able to articulate the relevance of its programs through word of mouth, distribution of pamphlets, and other methods of publicity.

Proximity studies over the past 25 years have demonstrated again and again the inverse relationship between rate of college attendance and distance from an institution (Koos, 1944a, 1944b; Daughtry and Hawk, 1958; Medsker and Trent, 1965). Investigations of the residence patterns of commuter college students invariably point up the fact that most students live within a very few miles of their institution (Baird, 1969; Coordinating Council for Higher Education, 1969; Willis, 1958, 1964). Educational and political leaders have begun to realize the validity and implication of statements such as the one President Kennedy made to Congress in 1963: "The opportunity for a college education is severely limited for hundreds of thousands of young people because there is no college in their own community" (O'Hara, 1966).

Geographic accessibility cannot be measured only in terms of minutes or miles; it must also be measured in terms of psychological obstacles which result partially from physical distance. For example, many students choose not to "go away to college" because it would mean disassociating themselves from old friends and familiar patterns of living in order to enter a world full of strangers.

For the middle-class student the problem is somewhat minimized because he is likely to be attending an institution where middle-class attitudes prevail, where middle-class English is the language of the professor, and where the majority of his fellow students are also from middle-class backgrounds. On the other hand, it is because of these same factors that the lower-class student (particularly the lower-class minority student) finds the proximity question more complex than simply the physical distance to be traveled. For him it may mean leaving one cultural setting (in which he is quite comfortable) for another (in which he is quite uncomfortable). It may mean being required to operate within a value or attitude structure that has in the past been unacceptable to him. It may mean reading, writing, and listening to a language in which he has never felt competent. It may mean attempting the difficult task of establishing social relations with students who have never lived in circumstances like his and who have concerns quite different from his own.[2] In short, he may have to leave his neighborhood and travel to a "foreign" institution, be it uptown, downtown, out of town, or out of state. While there would undoubtedly be other students whose backgrounds and interests were similar to his, the very fact that they would constitute and be treated as a minority group only highlights the implication that the institution operates primarily for other types of students.

A study of free-access higher education

The United States has committed itself, both individually as states and collectively as a nation, to further expansion of higher educational opportunity. Many national spokesmen, including former Secretary of Health, Education, and Welfare Robert H. Finch, have argued that expansion should not stop short of universal opportunity, that higher education should be accessible to all people (Jacobson, 1969). If the United States does adopt this more idealistic notion as a legitimate goal (and trends certainly indicate a definite movement in that direction), then it is necessarily obliged to take whatever steps it can to alleviate the financial, academic, motivational, and geographic barriers that still make higher education inaccessible to so many. The first and biggest step, according to educators, legislative leaders, administrative officials, and the educationally and economically disadvantaged men on the street, is that inexpensive institutions must be placed within commuting distance of all United States residents. But that is not sufficient. Such institutions must also develop programs that are relevant to the needs of a diverse population and flexible and encouraging in their dealings with nontraditional students.

---

2. Social psychologists have researched the question of social interaction and have concluded that people generally restrict most of their social relations to others with similar backgrounds. One of the most famous studies on the subject was conducted by Hollingshead and Warner in southern Illinois (Hollingshead, 1949).

This suggestion, of course, is not new, but it is being made with increasing fervor. The following three examples are indicative of the widespread concern. First, President Nixon has labeled expanded assistance to community colleges (the most common type of institution being called for) as one of the highest priorities of his administration, although his view that these institutions should serve almost exclusively a specialized career-training function is somewhat disturbing. Second, the Carnegie Commission on Higher Education recently called for the establishment of between 230 and 280 community colleges by 1980 to bring at least one such institution within commuting distance of 95 percent of the population[3] (Carnegie Commission, 1970b). Third, Senator Harrison A. Williams Jr., and 27 of his colleagues have proposed a $6 billion "comprehensive community college act" in which the federal government would allot funds to the states over a three year period starting in 1971. The purpose of such a bill, according to Williams, is "to assist the states in providing postsecondary education to all persons in all areas of each state" (*Higher Education and National Affairs*, 1969).

Many states are presently contemplating the establishment of more community colleges (Yarrington, 1969). Pennsylvania, for example, has identified 28 service areas for community colleges and is in the process of trying to equip as many as is feasible with at least one institution. Twelve areas are presently being served, with study under way in 10 of the remaining 16.

Purpose. One of the dangers of any program that calls for urgent action is the temptation to move ahead without adequately analyzing past activity. This is particularly true of expansion of higher educational opportunity. State planners often assume that certain types of institutions have provided opportunity for certain kinds and numbers of people in the past. Operating partially on that assumption, they decide to build or not to build more colleges in a given area. This study is intended to undergird (or in some cases, undermine) this assumption and thus contribute to a better understanding of the accessibility of higher education throughout the country by providing data pertinent to such questions as:

1. To what extent and in what ways has the degree of accessibility of institutions of higher education changed over the past decade?

2. To what extent has low-cost, nonselective higher education been made available to the general population over the past decade? To whites? Blacks? Mexican Americans? City dwellers? Suburban residents? Rural families?

3. How many low-cost, nonselective institutions have been constructed in various metropolitan areas and states within the past decade?

4. What effect has their construction had upon the status of access to higher education within these areas? What states and metropolitan areas have demonstrated the greatest gain? The least gain?

5. What factors have caused different rates of accessibility in different areas over the past 10 years, and what has been the relative importance of each?

---

3. This is a revision of their 1968 recommendation of 550 community colleges by 1976.

To look at the question of accessibility in terms of proximity is, of course, to consider only part of the problem. If one is to be intelligent in planning future courses of action, one must not only be aware of the demographic characteristics of areas served and not served by low-cost, nonselective institutions, but must also understand the extent to which such colleges actually profit the people who live within commuting distance. To say that a college is or is not in a given location populated by certain kinds of people, and to know the number of colleges established in given areas within the past decade are vital first steps, but to discern whether or not a college actually draws large numbers of local people, whether or not it has programs designed specifically to meet the needs of the community, and whether or not it has the physical and financial resources to accommodate those who desire higher education is equally important. The quantitative analyses of this study form a backdrop for subsequent investigations of such qualitative issues.

Methodology.[4] Warren Willingham, Senior Research Psychologist of the College Entrance Examination Board, recently completed a study of the accessibility of higher education as of fall 1968 (Willingham, 1970). He developed a wealth of data on the number and types of freely accessible institutions and also on the demographic characteristics of various populations within commuting distance of such institutions.

The availability of these data has afforded the opportunity to conduct an investigation with two main objectives: (1) the assessment of the growth in higher educational opportunity within geographic areas and population groups between 1958 and 1968, and (2) the examination and clarification of underlying factors instrumental in this growth. The first objective was met by gathering data for 1958 comparable to the data Willingham gathered for 1968; the second, by analyzing the two sets of data in terms of underlying factors that have affected higher educational opportunity in the decade 1958-1968.

In order to develop comparable data, the methodology employed in this study followed closely that of Willingham's study. Both studies were built upon the assumption that accessible higher education must have at least three characteristics. It must be relatively inexpensive, it must admit the majority of high school graduates, and it must exist in such proximity that neither geographical nor psychological distance constitute a major barrier.

Operating on this assumption, each college in the country was rated on a five-point scale based jointly on tuition and selectivity for both 1958 and 1968. Institutions that had annual tuition charges of no more than 5 percent of the national median family income ($230 in 1958, $400 in 1968) and that enrolled at least one-third of their freshmen from students in the bottom half of their high school classes were classified as "free-access" colleges. These colleges were then placed on maps with commuting perimeters around each.

---

4. A more extensive description of the research methodology used may be found in: Richard I. Ferrin, "An Analysis of the Changes in Free-Access Higher Education in the United States from 1958 to 1968." Unpublished doctoral dissertation, Stanford University, 1970, on file in the Access Research Office of the College Entrance Examination Board.

Based on results of previous studies and rules of thumb employed by state planning agencies, a one-way commuting guideline was used. This guideline was translated into variable commuting radii that ranged from 2.5 miles in the largest cities to 25 miles in small towns and rural areas.

Several changes altered the complexion of free-access higher education in the decade 1958-1968. New institutions opened, existing ones relocated, others closed, a few became too costly, while still others became too selective. Each category of colleges was dealt with separately in this study in order to assess the impact of each on the accessibility scene. Population estimates were made in terms of county, census tract, or Congressional district coverage, depending upon the population density of the area. And when proceeding from one category to the next, the only populations estimated were those living in portions of the commuting area not overlapping areas already counted. In other words, no person was counted twice.

This research deals with only one aspect of educational opportunity and as such provides only one type of input for educational planning. Those who would seek to expand such opportunity must regard these findings as providing answers to only a few of the questions that must be raised.

2. The changing character of college accessibility

Although the number of United States institutions enrolling freshmen increased substantially within the period 1958-1968 (from 1,890 to 2,596 institutions), there remains considerable question as to the nature of that growth. For example, many individuals suggest that low-cost, relatively nonselective higher education has become much more accessible to the general population in recent years. One index which tends to temper the enthusiasm behind such statements shows that whereas 1 out of every 3.5 institutions of higher education could be labeled "free-access" in 1958, the figure had improved only to 1 in 3.3 ten years later.

Can one infer, then, that only a handful of accessible institutions came into being in this decade? Obviously not. In fact, quite the contrary is true. Since 1958 the number of free-access colleges increased from 538 to 789, a growth of 47 percent. (Table 2.) At the same time, however, the number of non-free-access institutions also increased (from 1,352 to 1,807), thereby largely offsetting the statistical advance of the free-access group. Low-cost but academically selective public colleges and universities enjoyed the most vigorous numerical expansion as they more than doubled, but private institutions that were both costly and selective also expanded markedly.

Table 2. Development of various types of inaccessibility, 1958 and 1968

Type of inaccessibility	Public 1958	1968	Private 1958	1968	Total 1958	1968	Percent net change
Special purpose	11	11	68	93	79	104	+ 32
Religious emphasis	0	0	313	395	313	395	+ 26
Costly, not selective	40	50	274	262	314	312	− 1
Selective, not costly	132	341	14	15	146	356	+144
Both costly and selective	44	57	444	575	488	632	+ 30
Non-coed (not included above)	5	2	7	6	12	8	− 33
Total non-free-access	232	461	1,120	1,346	1,352	1,807	+ 34
Total free-access	499	772	39	17	538	789	+ 47
United States	731	1,233	1,159	1,363	1,890	2,596	+ 37

When one adds to these data the interesting fact that there was no increase (in fact, there was a rather insignificant decrease) in the number of costly, but nonselective institutions, it suggests that selectivity rather than cost has been the crucial factor in extending comparative inaccessibility to large numbers of colleges and universities since 1958. While tuition charges have increased at institutions of higher education in this period, their rate of increase in established institutions (those in existence in both 1958 and 1968) has tended to be only slightly more rapid than the increase in median family income. If one considers new institutions as well, the tuition picture is quite different from that generally accepted. In 1968 a far larger percentage of colleges (42 percent) had tuition charges below 5 percent of the median family income than in 1958 (28 percent). In fact about the same percentage charged $400 or less in 1968 as they did 10 years earlier. To put it another way, one must not let the image of the private college, whose average tuition increased from $550 to $1,170 in this period, obscure the fact that nearly half of all institutions in the nation are relatively inexpensive.

Selectivity is quite a different matter. Of the established institutions roughly one-third of those admitting large proportions of freshmen from the bottom half of high school classes in 1958 had become at least moderately selective 10 years later. More than 50 percent of this group admitted primarily students from the top-third of high school classes.

The most dramatic growth in both the free-access and non-free-access areas can be found within the public sector. The private sector entered this period with 428 more institutions than the public sector, but by 1968 that margin had been reduced to only 130. Moreover, what gain private institutions did make occurred exclusively within the non-free-access area. Where free-access private colleges accounted for 7 percent of all free-access institutions in 1958, they represented only 2 percent in 1968. Most private colleges and universities were judged inaccessible for both target years on either financial or religious grounds; 62 percent in 1958 and 61 percent in 1968 were too costly, and 27 percent and 29 percent, respectively, had a strong religious emphasis. Very few institutions were inaccessible solely on grounds of selectivity in either year.

Although the majority of public institutions in both 1958 and 1968 were freely accessible, the proportion dropped from 68 percent to 62 percent. At the same time, of course, the absolute number of such colleges had burgeoned. While this fact is well known and widely discussed, the subtle but significant change that has occurred within the selective, low-cost institutional category is much less understood. The number of these institutions, many of them state senior colleges and universities, increased approximately two-and-one-half times since 1958. Many senior institutions or state systems have either informally or formally concluded that it is the job of the expanding two-year colleges to provide mass postsecondary education while the four-year colleges admit only those students with superior academic credentials. The California three-tiered master plan is perhaps the most notable formal example of this approach, although others exist throughout the nation. To illustrate, almost half (32) of the 68 land-grant universities fell within the selective, low-cost category in 1968, with many more being both selective and costly. Only 15, on the other hand, qualified as free-access institutions.

According to Table 3 one can see that of the 538 free-access institutions in 1958, one-fifth (109) were disqualified in 1968 on grounds of selectivity although they were still relatively low-cost. Included in this group were 88 public senior colleges and universities, 12 public two-year colleges, 5 public two-

Table 3. Number of free-access institutions by existence type, 1958 and 1968

Free-access status	1958	1968
Free-access in 1958 and 1968, same location	361	361
Free-access in 1958 and 1968, changed locations	10	10
Free-access in 1958, too costly in 1968	18	—
Free-access in 1958, too selective in 1968	109	—
Free-access in 1958, too costly and too selective in 1968	12	—
Free-access in 1958, not in OFE* in 1968	28	—
Not free-access in 1958, free-access in 1968	—	28
New free-access colleges since 1968	—	390
United States	538	789

*Opening Fall Enrollment, an annual publication of the United States Office of Education.

year branches, and only 4 private institutions. The predominance once again of the state colleges and universities is simply another piece of evidence to support the conclusion that senior institutions are on the whole less accessible now than they were a decade ago.

By comparing figures from Tables 2 and 3, it is obvious that the first table conceals the extent to which new free-access colleges have cropped up since 1958. While Table 2 shows a net increase of 251, Table 3 indicates that there were actually 418 free-access institutions added between 1959 and 1968. Of this latter group 390 were actually new institutions that came into being as free-access colleges, while a handful existed in 1958 as non-free-access colleges. (Of this handful most had a cost figure in 1958 just a few dollars above the free-access limit but enacted only slight increases, if any, in the subsequent decade.) The difference between 418 and 251 (167) represents the number of colleges that were free-access in 1958 but not in 1968 — primarily because they became too selective.

Many free-access colleges changed locations between the two target years. For the purpose of this study, however, the effect of that movement was calculated for only those institutions that moved from one city to another, or for those in the central cities of large metropolitan areas (more than 500,000 population) that indicated any address change. This procedure is defensible in that the commuting radius is so large in a small city that a location change within its borders is not likely to have much affect on estimates of accessibility. On the other hand, a change of even a few blocks within a large city could have a marked affect upon that institution's accessibility to various population groups.

Somewhat surprisingly, a careful search uncovered only 10 institutions that underwent a location change as defined above. Of course, this analysis focused solely on two points in time, 1958 and 1968, and only on those institutions actually in temporary facilities or on old campuses *in 1958*. Colleges moving to new locations before 1959 and the rash of institutions, primarily public two-year colleges, that opened in temporary facilities after 1958 were not included. A large number of the latter have since moved to permanent campuses, but they show up in the data simply as new free-access institutions.

Changes by Institutional Type. Table 4 illustrates in general terms the nature of institutional growth between 1958 and 1968. As is commonly known, public two-year colleges exhibited the greatest numerical growth, increasing from 320 to 642.

In 1958 only 1 institution in 6 was a public two-year college, but by 1968 the proportion was 1 in 4. Forty-three of the 50 states established at least one such institution in this period, with many states opening several. As one would expect, California led the way with 26, followed by Illinois with 24, and New York and North Carolina with 22 each.

In addition to the increase in the number of two-year institutions, average enrollment in these colleges has risen from 600 to 1,100. These institutions serve an increasingly large proportion of the nation's new freshmen; for example,

Table 4. Changes in number of institutions, by type, 1958 and 1968 (percent of total institutions in parentheses)

Type	1958	1968	1958/1968 Ratio
Public:			
Two-year	320 (17%)	642 (25%)	2.0
Four-year	371 (20%)	433 (17%)	1.2
Branches	45 (2%)	159 (6%)	3.5
All private	1,154 (61%)	1,362 (53%)	1.2
United States	1,890	2,596	1.4

in 1958, slightly over 1 freshman in 5 attended a public two-year college, by 1968 nearly 2 in 5 did.

Expansion within four-year institutions was more moderate. As with all higher education, freshman enrollment swelled in senior colleges; in fact, it more than doubled as 655,000 first-time students entered in 1968 compared with 314,000 who entered 10 years earlier. Since not many new institutions were established, one can readily understand the marked increase in the number of freshmen at the average four-year college or university (846 in 1958 and 1,516 in 1968). This group of institutions probably more than any other has felt the pressures of overcrowding, which partially explains their movement up the selectivity ladder. Whether by design or by accident, many four-year institutions have chosen increased selectivity as a more feasible, and no doubt in some cases a more desirable, alternative to still further stretching and expansion of facilities.

The branch campus is a comparative newcomer to the higher education scene. A few states, such as Indiana, Ohio, and Pennsylvania have had well-established systems of branch institutions since the 1930s and 1940s, but most campuses were primarily evening school and/or adult education operations until the mid-1950s. As recently as 1958 only 14 states reported they had branch campuses that offered a full range of degree-credit courses. By 1968, however, 31 states reported such institutions. Many states, including California, Illinois, and Texas have rejected the branch approach to increased accessibility in favor of the creation of a system of two-year colleges and co-equal senior colleges and universities.

The figures in Table 4, showing the growth of branch campuses from 45 in 1958 to 159 in 1968, should be treated with caution because many institutions commonly known throughout their respective states as branch campuses have been reported to the United States Office of Education, and hence regarded in this study, as being on equal footing with the main campus. These institutions have been included with other four-year institutions, thereby causing branch campuses to be underrepresented.

As a group, branch campuses enrolled a very small proportion (1.0 percent) of all first-time students entering college in 1958 and showed only a slight increase in 1968 when they enrolled 2.7 percent of all freshmen. First-time enrollment at the average branch institution remained below 500 throughout the decade, a figure less than half the enrollment at public two-year colleges.

Finding it ever more difficult to compete with the public sector in this era of high costs, private institutions have been largely bypassed in the higher education growth of the 1960s. While one can point to isolated cases of institutions that have expanded considerably, the overall picture is not bright. Although more than 200 private colleges opened between 1958 and 1968 and although the majority of institutions in the United States continue to be private, fewer than 1 of 4 freshmen entered a private college in 1968. This marked a drop of 15 percent over the past decade.

Changes within accessibility levels

In both the Willingham study and this study, institutions were sorted into one of five levels of accessibility based on costs and selectivity. Because there have been institutional changes from one level to another and because colleges have both opened and closed during the period 1958-1968, it seems appropriate to present a brief profile of each level. Institutions considered "free-access" are those that fall in levels 1 and 2.

Level 1. Institutions at this level are popularly regarded as being "open-door." Tuition is free or quite low, and all high school graduates are accepted for admission. In 1958 there were 151 such institutions; by 1968 that number had swelled to 282. As presented in Table 5, public two-year colleges constituted the greatest proportion in both years, with their absolute number more than doubling during the decade. Public four-year college representation was reduced sharply during this period, although the branch campuses of such institutions increased from two to ten. The number of private institutions represented was very small, and together they enrolled only a handful of freshmen. Public two-year colleges, on the other hand, enrolled 123,000 freshmen in 1958 and burgeoned to an enrollment of 375,000 freshmen in 1968. (Table 6.) Overall, institutions at this level enrolled 1 out of 6 freshmen in 1958 and 1 out of 5 in 1968.

Table 5. Number of colleges in the United States by accessibility level and type, 1958 and 1968

| Type | Accessibility level (1958) | | | | | Total |
	1	*2*	*3*	*4*	*5*	*Total*
Public:						
Two-year	129	154	31	6	0	320
Four-year	17	186	96	72	0	371
Branches	2	12	24	7	0	45
All private	3	35	172	831	113	1,154
United States	151	387	323	916	113	1,890

| Type | Accessibility level (1968) | | | | | Total |
	1	*2*	*3*	*4*	*5*	*Total*
Public:						
Two-year	262	332	34	13	1	642
Four-year	8	127	134	90	74	433
Branches	10	33	104	7	5	159
All private	2	15	117	914	314	1,362
United States	282	507	389	1,024	394	2,596

Level 2. Institutions at this level may be classified as almost open-door. Their tuition charges, though higher than those at level 1, are still relatively modest and within the reach of most students not clearly in a poverty situation. They accept most high school graduates, and as Willingham stated, "what little selecting they practice is usually directed to screening students in the bottom quarter of the high school class — often because of lack of space rather than a specific policy of selective admissions." This level of accessibility, like level 1, has become virtually the domain of the public sector. There were fewer public four-year colleges in 1968 than in 1958, but the public two-year college group more than doubled and in 1968 comprised two-thirds of all level 2 institutions.

Level 3. As Willingham has put it, "this is the first level to which a substantial number of high school graduates may experience difficulty in gaining access. If the scholastic requirement is not a barrier, then the higher tuition may be." There was relatively little numerical growth in the number of these institutions between 1958 and 1968 (323 to 398), but there was a great deal of change within the category. Where the private college was the typical level 3 institution in 1958, the public four-year college had assumed that position a decade later. In the 10-year period, 72 of these institutions moved to this level of moderate inaccessibility. Of course, during the same time quite a few public four-year colleges moved from level 3 to become even less accessible to the general student population.

Two-thirds of the 159 branch campuses were situated at this level in 1968. This fact is interesting in light of a widely held opinion that the raison d'être for the branch campus is to provide local higher education to any high school graduate who desires it. Ohio, for example, which takes pride in the extent to which higher education has been made geographically accessible through its large system of branch institutions, had no branch campus at either level 1 or 2 in 1968 but rather had 26 of its 28 institutions at level 3. While these campuses are indeed accessible to a large proportion of high school graduates, there are many who because of lack of funds and/or unsatisfactory academic credentials are barred from admittance. Ohio is only one of several states confronted with this situation. Most of these states, including Ohio, have evidently realized that certain groups, such as minority/poverty students, often are not reached through the branches and now have begun to establish independent two-year institutions.

Private colleges accounted for more than half the level 3 institutions in 1958, but in the course of the following decade they, like the public four-year colleges, became even less accessible. Approximately 50 private colleges left this level, some because they ceased to function but most because their costs and/or admissions requirements became too stringent.

The proportion of all freshmen enrolling in level 3 colleges decreased

Table 6. First-time enrollment by accessibility level and institutional type, 1958 and 1968 (in thousands)

| Type | Accessibility level (1958) | | | | | Total |
	1	2	3	4	5	
Public:						
Two-year	123	57	17	1	—	199
Four-year	12	146	94	62	—	314
Branches	—	2	5	1	—	8
All private	—	11	45	221	54	331
United States	136*	216	160*	286*	54	852

| Type | Accessibility level (1968) | | | | | Total |
	1	2	3	4	5	
Public:						
Two-year	375	310	45	7	2	739
Four-year	7	146	210	138	146	647
Branches	6	9	31	2	1	49
All private	1	5	32	254	155	447
United States	389	470	318	401	304	1,882

* Detail does not add to total because of rounding.

slightly over the 10-year period (from 19 percent to 17 percent). Of those who did enroll, the majority attended public four-year colleges in both 1958, when there were almost twice as many private institutions as public four-year colleges, and in 1968 when the public institutions predominated.

Level 4. In 1958, prior to the establishment of such a host of public institutions and prior to the great influx of students from the lower income and achievement groups, 1 out of 3 freshmen attended institutions at this level of relative inaccessibility. Most of them matriculated at one of the 831 private colleges, but 22 percent did enroll in 1 of the 72 public four-year colleges at this level. The primary growth in number of institutions between 1958 and 1968 occurred within the private sector, while the public four-year colleges bore the brunt of the enrollment increase as their average entering class size nearly doubled. Private institutions, which included a large number of special purpose and strongly religious colleges, remained small with virtually no change in their total enrollment.

Level 5. In 1958 the only institutions at this highly selective and costly level were the nation's 113 major private universities and elite liberal arts colleges. No public institution was included since none charged as high as $920 tuition nor did any restrict admission to only those from the top 10 to 15 percent of their high school class. During the sixties, however, the scene changed considerably. By 1968, while the private sector still dominated, 80 public colleges and universities had also become highly selective. Most of the 80 were prestigious state colleges and universities, with California and New York together accounting for 32.

Enrollments grew nearly sixfold as the institutions at this level recorded the largest jump in the proportion of the student population attending. In 1958 only 1 freshman in 16 entered a level 5 institution, but by 1968, 1 in 6 matriculated at this level. Despite being greatly outnumbered, the public sector enrolled nearly as many students as the private sector. The average freshman class at a four-year public college or university was 2,000, approximately four times as large as its private counterpart.

Changes within regions

Willingham pointed out that in 1968 there were striking differences between regions regarding accessibility. He noted and his data illustrated that the West was far ahead of any other region in the proportion of free-access colleges and in the proportion of the regional enrollment attending those colleges. He found that half of all Western colleges in 1968 were free-access, and that 71 percent of all new freshmen in the region were enrolled in such institutions. He further indicated that the Northeast was as far below the national average as the West was above it. Only 14 percent of all Northeastern colleges were free-access, and enrolled only 1 out of 5 first-time students.

One should not infer from these findings, however, that institutional planners in the Northeast had fallen asleep on the question of the accessibility of higher education during the sixties or that their counterparts in the West had awakened. Indeed, as observers of the collegiate admissions scene are well aware, the opposite, while put too strongly, may be closer to what took place. As Table 7 illustrates, in 1958 the Northeast had only 29 free-access institutions (none were completely open-door), of which nine were in New England. These 29 constituted a mere 6 percent of all institutions in the region and enrolled only 1 out of 20 freshmen attending college in the Northeast. In 1968 there were 92 free-access colleges enrolling more than 1 out of 5 freshmen attending college in the region.

At the other end of the continuum the West, led by California, has for many years been the envy of educational leaders in other regions who have tried to

Table 7. Number and percentage of institutions that were free-access in 1958 and 1968, by region

	1958			1968		
	Free-access	All institutions	Percent free-access	Free-access	All institutions	Percent free-access
Region						
Northeast	29	469	6%	92	647	14%
Midwest	164	562	29	193	740	26
South	216	595	36	312	821	38
West	129	264	49	192	388	49
United States	538	1,890	28%	789	2,596	30%

expand their own systems of free-access higher education. In 1958 more than 80 percent of the West's public institutions were free-access, including practically all its two-year colleges. Even when private institutions were added, 1 out of 2 colleges in the region was free-access. Seventy-three percent of all freshmen were enrolled in such institutions, a figure well above the national average.

The situation in the West 10 years later was virtually the same. Very little growth had taken place. A group of more than 60 new free-access colleges had come into existence, of course, but their affect had been partially diminished by several state colleges becoming accessible. Where in 1958 half of all public four-year colleges had been free-access, by 1968 that ratio had been reduced to less than 1 out of 3. Also, there had been little change in the percentage of all first-time students who matriculated at a free-access college (73 percent to 71 percent). This lack of growth would not at first glance seem to cause any concern because available data indicated that the West is still leading all other regions by a wide margin. There is a fly in the ointment, however, particularly in California. On the one hand, most people in this state have become used to the idea that free higher education is open to any high school graduate. On the other, residents in recent years have begun to balk at requests for additional funds necessary for expansion. Many feel that the system is currently large enough to take care of the area's postsecondary education needs. The problem arises from the fact that between 1958 and 1968 the percentage of 18-year-olds who graduated from high school increased from 61 percent to 77 percent, almost double the national increase. Since institutional growth has not matched the increase in "qualified" applicants, considerable overcrowding has resulted and there are many high school graduates living in areas, both urban and rural, not adequately serviced by free-access institutions. At issue in California and throughout the West is not whether it can remain ahead of the national average regarding accessibility but whether it can and will live up to the expectations that have been engendered by past performances.

The Midwest has traditionally been turned to by those who wish to get a reading on what the average American is eating, thinking, or doing. Educators have also looked to this region again and again as a barometer in matters of educational practice. In the matter of college accessibility one finds that in 1958 the Midwest mirrored very well what was going on around the nation. It had practically the same proportion of free-access colleges among its institutional population as the national average (29 percent and 28 percent, respectively, according to Table 7). It also had nearly the same percentage of its freshmen enrolled in free-access colleges (37 percent and 41 percent, respectively). Also, the distribution of free-access institutions throughout the various colleges and universities is closer to the national average than that of any other region.

By 1968, however, the Midwest was below the national average, both in proportion of free-access colleges and in proportion of students enrolling in such institutions. Between 1958 and 1968 the region showed an increase of only 29 free-access institutions. Like other regions this resulted from a host of new public two-year colleges coming into existence (60) counteracted by about 30 public four-year institutions becoming less accessible. In 1958, 65 percent of the Midwest's state senior institutions were considered free-access, but in 1968 only 26 percent were. No other region had as large a reduction in this kind of institution, although every region did show a decrease.

Like the West, the proportion of students enrolling in free-access colleges in the Midwest remained relatively static. In both 1958 and 1968 approximately one-third of all first-time students attended such an institution, but this occurred while the national average increased from 41 percent to 46 percent.

The South, which stretches from Delaware to Texas, not only had the largest population but also the most free-access colleges of any region in the nation in 1958 (216). One out of every 3 institutions was free-access, and they were attended by one-half of all freshmen entering college in the South. This was the only region with more free-access public four-year institutions than public two-year ones (102 to 81). Although 41 of the former became too selective to be included in 1968, several new ones were added. The South continued to offer low-cost, relatively nonselective higher education in nearly half of its 217 public four-year colleges and branch campuses, the only region to have such a high proportion.

Of course, when one considers the question of college accessibility in the South, mention must be made of the de facto racial segregation that still exists in many institutions. Although it is difficult to determine the extent of its effect, one can state without fear of contradiction that the statistics presented in this study overstate for both 1958 and 1968 the degree to which higher education is accessible in the South. In many areas two free-access institutions serve approximately the same geographical area, one catering primarily to the white population and the other to the black.

Changes by type of community

Since the majority of all colleges and universities are still under private control, it is not surprising that almost half of all institutions in 1958 and 42 percent in 1968 were located in counties with a population of less than 50,000. Much of this placement was determined in the last century when educational leaders felt the further they were able to keep students from the evils of the city the better. Both then and now the relative cost of land has also weighed heavily in the decision to establish institutions in less crowded suburbs and rural areas.

Although both of the above factors (as well as numerous others) remain strong considerations when planning construction of a college, be it public or private, it is nevertheless surprising that the large majority of free-access colleges in both 1958 and 1968 were situated in small towns and nonmetropolitan areas. One might assume that such institutions, largely supported as they are by tax funds, would be strategically located so as to place opportunity for higher education within reach of the largest number of people. Further, since a large proportion of those in poverty live in large cities, one might also expect that colleges that are low-cost or even tuition-free would be established in these areas. A glance at the data in Tables 8 and 9, however, reveals just the opposite. In 1958 two-thirds of all free-access colleges were located in counties with a population of under 50,000; by 1968 (after unusual expansion of community colleges), more than half still were. In both years approximately 4 out of 10 colleges in these small counties were free-access.

At the other end of the population scale, central cities in the major (more than one million population) metropolitan areas of the nation had only 5 percent of all free-access colleges in 1958 and 8 percent in 1968. In 1958 this meant that there were only 26 free-access colleges in the 14 largest cities in the United States; Los Angeles and Chicago had eight each. Such cities as New York, Philadelphia, Detroit, and Boston did not have even one. Although the situation improved during the subsequent decade, six major cities were still without a free-access college in 1968. Even with this improvement 85 percent of all colleges and universities in these central cities of areas with more than a million residents (in 1968 there were 29) were non-free-access and hence generally unavailable to many local residents.

Fringe areas of these largest cities exhibited the sharpest increase in the number of free-access colleges between 1958 and 1968. In 1958 only 6 percent of all free-access institutions were situated there; in 10 years the percentage had doubled. As Willingham has stated: "suburban colleges [in 1968] are almost twice as likely to be free-access [as urban colleges] despite the pressing social problems in the central cities and the fact that urban populations are less likely to be educationally mobile" (Willingham, 1970b). It is also interesting to note that the central cities gained 34 free-access colleges; the fringe areas gained 63. (Table 9.) The next two chapters will report data showing relative population coverage by free-access colleges for both 1958 and 1968, and these findings should bring into sharper focus the extent to which higher educational resources have been made accessible to residents of various geographic and demographic areas.

Table 8. Percentage distribution of free-access and non-free-access colleges by type of community, 1958 and 1968

	Percent free-access		Percent non-free-access		Total colleges	
Type of community	1958	1968	1958	1968	1958	1968
Metropolitan areas (1,000,000+)						
Central city	10	15	90	85	266	402
Fringe	17	29	83	71	196	337
Metropolitan areas (500,000 to 999,000)	16	20	84	80	151	259
Metropolitan areas (50,000 to 499,000)	23	30	77	70	416	509
Counties under 50,000	42	39	58	61	861	1,089

Table 9. Percentage distribution of free-access colleges by type of community, 1958 and 1968

			Total free-access colleges	
Type of community	1958	1968	1958	1968
Metropolitan areas (1,000,000+)				
Central city	5%	8%	26	60
Fringe	6	12	33	96
Metropolitan areas (500,000 to 999,000)	4	7	24	54
Metropolitan areas (50,000 to 499,000)	17	19	94	153
Counties under 50,000	67	54	361	426
United States	100%*	100%	538	789

* Detail does not add to total because of rounding.

3. Colleges are for people

Knowledge of the changing character of college accessibility is necessary to an understanding of the problems attendant to expanding educational opportunity, but it is not sufficient. To say that 538 free-access colleges existed in the United States in 1958 and 789 existed in 1968 is worth knowing, but other data are necessary if one is to see the relationship between these readily accessible colleges and the people they are designed to serve.

This chapter will present a picture of the extent to which free-access higher education was made available to various demographic, ethnic, and geographic groups between 1958 and 1968. Chapter 4 will discuss some of the factors that have been instrumental in this growth (or lack of it).

Before reporting any findings, it is worth while underscoring a methodological point. The particular estimates reported are fallible in the sense that different definitions of accessibility yield varying estimates of population coverage by free-access institutions. If tuition or selectivity limits were changed to include or exclude certain colleges, obviously there would be a corresponding change in the number of people considered to be within reasonable commuting distance of free-access higher education. The essential point to remember, however, is that these estimates are useful only to the extent that they convey general impressions of what has occurred among various population groups, within geographic regions, and in communities of different sizes. If one chooses to interpret the data as precise indices of the degree of college accessibility within particular situations, he has successfully missed the point of this study.

As was documented in the previous chapter, the opportunities to attend a low-cost, relatively nonselective college have expanded in the past decade. By 1968 roughly 42 percent of the nation's population lived within commuting distance of such institutions. While advocates of universal higher education might wish that the percentage were much higher, one would do well to note that in 1958 the corresponding figure was only 30 percent. To put this growth another way, more than 75 million people lived near the 789 free-access institutions in 1968 as compared with fewer than 46 million who lived within commuting distance of the 538 institutions a decade earlier. When these facts are coupled with the acknowledged national increase in college aspirations resulting in large part from the demands of an ever more complex society (Trow, 1970), it is little wonder that freshman enrollments at free-access colleges jumped 144 percent during this same period.

Changes by type of community

In 1958 there was only moderate variation among communities of different sizes as to the percentage of their respective populations living within commuting distance of a free-access college. Residents of small metropolitan areas of 50,000 to 250,000 were somewhat more likely to be "covered" and residents of the major central cities in the nation somewhat less likely. (Table 10.) Fringe areas of major cities tended to have slightly better coverage than the cities themselves, but both, along with the very small counties, had less than a quarter of their respective populations "covered."

Table 10. Percentage of the population within commuting distance of a free-access college, by type of community, 1958 and 1968

Type of community	Percentage within commuting distance		
	1958	1968	Net increase
Metropolitan areas (SMSA)*			
1,000,000+	22	37	15
Central cities	(21)	(38)	(17)
Fringe areas	(24)	(37)	(13)
500,000 to 999,000	33	38	5
250,000 to 499,000	32	48	16
50,000 to 249,000	39	63	24
Counties not in SMSA			
20,000+	36	48	12
Under 20,000	22	24	2
United States	30	42	12

* Standard Metropolitan Statistical Areas

Perhaps inevitably, the situation in small counties was virtually unchanged a decade later. As indicated in Table 11, both the population and the number of free-access colleges had remained relatively stable, resulting in no appreciable increase in coverage. To significantly increase the proportion in these rural, sparsely populated areas would have required a host of small colleges literally strung out across the countryside. For several reasons, including the problems of the urban areas, such expenditures were evidently not deemed justifiable in light of the limited resources available. As the 1970s begin, proposals calling for more free-access institutions regrettably but understandably continue to slight rural areas. One notable example is a recent recommendation by the Carnegie Commission calling for community colleges or equivalent facilities to be established "within commuting range of potential students in all populous areas" (Carnegie Commission, 1970).

All other areas increased their coverage, however, with small metropolitan areas exhibiting the greatest growth, followed by major cities and intermediate metropolitan areas. One can readily understand why the small metropolitan areas jumped from 39 percent to 63 percent coverage in just 10 years when one realizes that about 30 areas with no free-access colleges in 1958 each opened one such institution within the ensuing decade. Because these areas often consist of moderately compact pockets of population separated from larger areas and each other by expansive rural lands (Texas is an excellent example of this demographic phenomenon), one institution is within commuting distance of a large proportion of an area's residents. Normally the college has been established in or near the largest city in the area, and because the city is not overly congested, both the city dwellers and many of those living on the outskirts can easily travel the necessary distance in 30 to 45 minutes.

Table 11. Distribution of free-access colleges, by type of community, 1958 and 1968

Type of community	Population change (percent)	Number of institutions 1958	Number of institutions 1968	Net increase
Metropolitan areas (SMSA)*				
1,000,000+	+48	59	156	97
Central cities.	(+30)	(26)	(60)	(34)
Fringe areas .	(+71)	(33)	(96)	(63)
500,000 to 999,000	+64	24	54	30
250,000 to 499,000	+11	39	61	22
50,000 to 249,000 .	+24	55	92	37
Counties not in (SMSA)*				
20,000+.	− 9	171	214	43
Under 20,000.	−12	190	212	22
United States.	+18	538	789	251

* Standard Metropolitan Statistical Areas

Unfortunately, the same is not true for the nation's major cities. Because of the population density and the resultant problems of limited mobility, the reasonable commuting area of a college in a large city is much less than in a city of 50 or 100 thousand. Thus it would take several strategically placed institutions to achieve the same population coverage in large cities as could be achieved with only a single college in a small city. While several of these major cities did in fact establish multiple colleges, at least nine added only one while 13 failed to add any. To repeat a finding from Willingham's study, "of the 29 metropolitan areas which now [in 1968] have a population of more than one million, Atlanta, Boston, Buffalo, Cincinnati, Detroit, and Paterson-Clifton-Passaic do not have any free-access college located within their city limits." This means that any of the more than four million residents of these cities who wanted to attend a free-access college were required to commute outside the city, an experience often complicated by residency requirements, insufficiency of public transportation beyond the city limits and, in some cases, by the dearth of institutions even in the fringe areas.

In 1958 half of all metropolitan areas of 500,000 to one million people were without any free-access colleges at all. Ten years later one-quarter still had none, and another one-quarter had only one. In fact two-thirds of the 35 medium-size metropolitan areas have either failed to establish any free-access colleges since 1958 or have established only one. For the most part taxpayers and decision-makers have attempted to meet their higher educational needs primarily through institutions in existence since the 1950s.

Many of these areas do have public institutions in their midst, and although they typically are now moderately inaccessible, the attitude may be that it would be an unnecessary duplication of facilities to create any new colleges. Two examples of this situation are Columbus, with Ohio State University but no free-access colleges, and Salt Lake City, with the University of Utah but no free-access colleges. In a few other places, such as Jersey City, the public institution has ceased to be free-access within the past decade, and efforts to meet the educational needs of many of those previously served so far have failed to result in the establishment of any new free-access college.

Changes in racial coverage

Traditionally, whites have earned a much higher annual wage than nonwhites, and the pattern in recent years is no exception. According to the Census Bureau, in 1968 the median family income was 40 percent lower for blacks than for whites (United States Bureau of the Census, 1969). It does not seem illogical to conjecture that the brown population, in this study consisting of Mexican Americans in the five Southwestern states and Puerto Ricans in New York and Chicago, fared approximately the same as blacks (United States Bureau of the Census, 1970). Given this situation, it would seem appropriate that free-access colleges should be more geographically accessible to blacks and browns than they are to whites. In actual fact this generally was the case both in 1958 and 1968, although browns showed no increase in population coverage over that period while blacks and whites benefited about equally. By 1968 roughly 1 out of 2 blacks and browns lived within commuting distance of a free-access college, while 42 percent of all whites did.

As indicated in Table 12, blacks and whites living in small metropolitan areas and browns living on the outskirts of very large urban areas had the best chance of living near a free-access institution in 1968 (70 percent, 62 percent, and 68 percent, respectively). Residents of rural counties, regardless of race, had the worst chance (24 percent, 27 percent, and 13 percent, respectively).

Although the amount of coverage did increase for the total population in communities of all sizes, it is worth remembering that the population in all but the smallest cities and rural areas also increased. The result was that the total population growth was only slightly less than the change in coverage; therefore, almost as many people were without opportunity for free-access higher education in 1968 as there were in 1958.

States have responded in varying degrees and at different times to the issue of accessibility. Some states, such as California, Connecticut, and Mississippi, have provided readily accessible higher education to half or more of their residents—black, white, and in the case of California, brown—since before 1958. Eight others, including six Southern states plus Illinois and Washington,

Table 12. Percentage of the population within commuting distance of a free-access college, by race and type of community, 1958 and 1968

Type of community	White			Black			Brown		
	1958	*1968*	*Change*	*1958*	*1968*	*Change*	*1958*	*1968*	*Change*
Metropolitan areas (SMSA)*									
1,000,000+	22	36	+14	25	40	+15	37	50	+13
Central cities	(20)	(36)	(+16)	(25)	(42)	(+17)	(24)	(42)	(+18)
Fringe areas	(24)	(37)	(+13)	(22)	(31)	(+ 9)	(63)	(68)	(+ 5)
500,000 to 999,000	32	36	+ 4	31	46	+15	67	66	− 1
250,000 to 499,000	31	47	+16	47	61	+14	51	37	−14
50,000 to 249,000	39	62	+23	45	70	+25	48	56	+ 8
Counties not in SMSA									
20,000+	35	48	+13	36	52	+16	56	42	−14
Under 20,000	22	24	+ 2	24	27	+ 3	31	13	−18
United States	29	42	+13	33	47	+14	48	47	− 1

_____

* Standard Metropolitan Statistical Areas

have attained this level of opportunity more recently. On the other hand, a few states, most notably Indiana, still offer virtually no free-access higher education to any of its residents. These states generally do have systems of moderately accessible institutions serving large proportions of high school graduates, but many young people are still left out for one reason or another.

Illinois and Missouri are two of a dozen states which in 1968 placed accessible institutions within reach of a higher proportion of blacks than whites. In these two states much of the credit goes to the expansive community college systems established in Chicago and St. Louis. Chicago, with more than three-fourths of the blacks in the state living within its city limits, located its campuses so as to provide accessible educational opportunities to more than 60 percent of these black residents. Through judicious campus placement the St. Louis system has been even more successful and has established free-access higher education within commuting distance of almost 80 per cent of the blacks in its city.

To leave the impression that the complete story of higher educational opportunity among races can be told by means of relatively straightforward quantitative data would be to perform a real disservice to anyone seeking understanding of this complex matter. Chapter 1 attempted to elucidate some of the more subtle problems that affect patterns of college attendance, particularly among nonwhites. Discrimination along racial lines still exists, more overtly in some states than others, despite the fact that most institutions have now signed the federal Assurance of Compliance with the Civil Rights Act of 1964. As Wiggins has stated: "At times this [discrimination] is because of hostile community attitudes. In other cases, the white institution's unwritten policy is to 'discourage' Negro applicants, or to limit their number. In some desegregated institutions, the policy is one of reluctant, even grudging admissions" (Wiggins, 1966). The issue is one that must be of grave national and local concern, but attempts to quantify it at this time cannot defensibly go beyond the conclusion that estimates of nonwhite coverage are generally inflated and in some states substantially so.

The reverse situation, that of white students enrolling in historically Negro institutions, is also camouflaged by the statistics of racial coverage so far presented. Willingham employed statistics to outline the magnitude of this problem when he analyzed the extent of white coverage in the South in 1968. First including predominately Negro institutions, and then excluding them he found only a modest difference of 3 percent (50 percent to 47 percent). Thus, although certain white students may be restrained from attending a nearby Negro college because the taboo of the mores is overpowering, almost all of these students have a white or integrated free-access college within commuting distance.

Changes within regions

Some of the general impressions that may be gleaned from the section on regional changes in the previous chapter are:

1. The West, despite only moderate growth during the past decade, continued to lead the other regions in the extent to which accessible institutions were available to and utilized by its residents;

2. The South, by using several types of free-access colleges (including community colleges, senior institutions, and technical education centers), slightly closed the gap between itself and the West;

3. The Midwest remained relatively static and actually lost ground in many areas; and

4. The Northeast, which had virtually no free-access colleges in 1958, made the most progress of any region, but still trailed all others by a wide margin. The data to be presented in this section show the relationship between colleges and people. The results will reinforce some but modify other of these impressions based only on number of colleges.

Table 13 illustrates the regional increases in the proportion of people within commuting range of an accessible institution between 1958 and 1968. The West was clearly the leader and the Northeast clearly the tailrunner a decade ago, but by 1968 the South had virtually the same degree of population coverage as the West, and the Northeast had improved enough to pass the Midwest. In both the South and West, then, 1 out of every 2 persons was within commuting distance of a free-access college in 1968; in the Northeast and Midwest approximately 1 out of 3 was.

Northeast. Although the growth of free-access higher education in the Northeast has been great in the past decade, it certainly was not unexpected. With the public sector in other regions assuming an ever-increasing obligation for the education of their youth, politicians and educators in the Northeast were bound to feel some pressure to provide opportunities for higher educa-

Table 13. Changes in the percentage of regional populations within commuting distance of a free-access college, by race, 1958 and 1968

| Region | Percentage within commuting distance | | | | | | | |
| | White | | Black | | Brown | | Total | |
	1958	1968	1958	1968	1958	1968	1958	1968
Northeast	15	38	7	37	—	36	15	38
Midwest	30	33	35	39	—	—	31	33
South	35	50	36	52	60	40	36	50
West	43	51	52	48	45	55	44	51
United States	29	42	33	47	48	47	30	42

— Base too small for reliable estimate

tion for those with average academic credentials but below-average financial resources. In the 1950s the student with either adequate finances or who demonstrated superior academic ability could find at least one of the many private colleges to which he could gain admittance, but the student who possessed neither was for the most part "left out in the cold." The pervasiveness of the private college syndrome throughout the region must absorb much of the responsibility for the delayed development of accessible public institutions. Legislators were slow, and in several states continue to be slow, to appropriate funds for free-access institutions. They prefer in many cases to give money to non-free-access (often private) colleges and universities to establish special programs for nontraditional, high-risk students. Parents generally regarded education in the few (29) free-access colleges that did exist in 1958 to be of very inferior quality, and high school seniors planning to attend college too often regarded such institutions as last resorts, as colleges to look toward when all hope of attending any other college was gone. To illustrate the extent to which students stayed away from these institutions, only four free-access colleges in the entire Northeast had freshman enrollments as large as 500 in 1958, and only 5 percent of all students attending college in the Northeast that year matriculated at a free-access institution.

Of course, one main reason why students did not attend these colleges was that they were geographically inaccessible to the large majority of the population. Only seven institutions were located in metropolitan areas of one-half million or more, yet almost three-fourths of the region's people lived in those areas. The central cities of New York, Boston, Philadelphia, and Pittsburgh were without even one such college, despite the fact that more than half of the region's black people lived in these four cities. In fact, throughout the Northeast a white student had twice as good a chance of living within commuting distance of a free-access college as did a black student (15 percent to 7 percent). Also, since virtually all the region's Puerto Ricans lived in New York City, they were completely beyond the range of an accessible institution.

It was inevitable that such a situation would eventually improve, and it has.

The City University of New York established four free-access campuses between 1958 and 1968, and its City Community College, slightly too costly in 1958, held its tuition charge stable and joined the ranks of accessible institutions in 1968. Roughly 3 out of 10 white New Yorkers were within commuting distance of one or more of these five campuses in 1968, but only 2 out of 10 black New Yorkers were. To put it another way, the overwhelming majority of the city's nearly eight million residents continued without free-access higher education as here defined and it was perhaps "kismetic" that the cry for open admissions that came in 1969 would be the loudest and most vehement there.

Newark, Philadelphia, and Pittsburgh have each established a single community college, but in every case it has been strategically located so as to be particularly accessible to black residents. The most dramatic example of the three is Newark. In 1958 only a relative handful of black residents was within commuting distance of a free-access college located on the outskirts, but a decade later almost 95 percent of the black population was within reach of the new centrally located institution. More than two-thirds of Newark's white residents were also within its commuting area. In the other two cities almost half the blacks and about three-tenths of the whites had a low-cost, nonselective college accessible to them in 1968; 10 years earlier no one did.

The situation in Boston, on the other hand, did not improve appreciably. In 1958 and again in 1968 few of the city's three-fourths of a million residents, black or white, lived near a free-access institution. Massachusetts had established several community colleges throughout the state between 1960 and 1968, but none are now in Boston. One community college was established in the city in 1961, but it has since moved to the suburbs, leaving New England's largest city without free-access higher educational opportunities.

Table 14. Changes in the percentage of different populations within commuting distance of a free-access college, by region, 1958 and 1968

| | Percentage within commuting distance | | | | | | | |
| | Northeast | | Midwest | | South | | West | |
Community type	1958	1968	1958	1968	1958	1968	1958	1968
Metropolitan Areas (SMSA)*								
1,000,000+	8	28	29	37	34	38	52	54
Central cities	(4)	(29)	(34)	(44)	(37)	(38)	(43)	(44)
Fringe areas	(14)	(27)	(20)	(30)	(29)	(38)	(61)	(62)
500,000 to 999,000	3	38	37	12	34	53	40	55
250,000 to 499,000	23	49	35	39	38	53	35	48
50,000 to 249,000	34	71	32	47	46	71	50	61
Counties not in SMSA								
20,000+	24	51	34	35	38	55	48	50
Under 20,000	8	24	20	23	25	28	16	17
United States	15	38	31	33	36	50	44	51

* Standard Metropolitan Statistical Areas

In summary, the Northeast has expanded its free-access facilities and population coverage greatly throughout the region and in communities of all sizes. (Table 14.) Also, according to Table 15, every state was in a better position in 1968 than in 1958, with the exception of Maine, which could not lay claim to even one such college in either year. The state leaders in the drive toward universal access to higher education were Connecticut, which in 1968 led the nation by placing a free-access college within commuting distance of 87 percent of its residents, and New York, which during the decade established the largest number of new accessible institutions in the region (26) and provided new free-access coverage to more than five million persons.

Table 15. Percentage of different population groups within commuting distance of a free-access college, by state, 1958 and 1968 — Northeast region

| State | Percentage within commuting distance | | | | | | | |
| | White | | Black | | Puerto Rican | | Total | |
	1958	1968	1958	1968	1958	1968	1958	1968
Connecticut	52	87	57	90	—	—	52	87
Maine	0	0	—	0	—	—	0	0
Massachusetts	25	45	18	23	—	—	24	52
New Hampshire	0	44	—	—	—	—	0	44
New Jersey	29	36	26	90	—	—	29	39
New York	9	38	1	23	0	36	7	36
Pennsylvania	9	24	4	41	—	—	9	25
Rhode Island	0	40	0	60	—	—	0	41
Vermont	27	41	—	—	—	—	27	41
Regional average	15	38	7	37	0	36	15	38
National average	29	42	33	47	48	47	30	42

— Base too small for reliable estimate

Despite this growth the Northeast established fewer new free-access colleges than any other region and remains behind two of the other three regions in proportion of the population covered. There is much that needs to be accomplished, and as is well known, it needs to begin in the central cities of the largest metropolitan areas.

Midwest. The Midwest, with its population more evenly distributed among communities of various sizes than is true of the Northeast, provided roughly one-third of its residents with a free-access college within commuting distance in both 1958 and 1968. Although considerable changes have occurred in various communities in the past decade, the Midwest as a whole made scant progress in expanding free-access opportunities, and through its inactivity has fallen behind all other regions. During the time other regions were averaging an increase of between five and seven free-access colleges per state, the heartland of the nation averaged less than half that number. In 1958, those living in rural counties and in the fringe areas of the largest cities, together accounting for approximately one-fourth of the region's population, were less fortunate than other residents; only 20 percent of each were within range of an accessible institution. The population of rural counties actually decreased in the following decade, and those areas continued to have coverage well below the regional average. Fringe areas of major cities, on the other hand, were the recipients of both a few million new residents and a score of new free-access colleges, and by 1968 they had increased their coverage to virtually match the regional average. These areas were predominantly white, and whites were the primary beneficiaries of this growth.

The most dramatic change took place in areas with 500,000 to one million residents. These areas led all communities in coverage with 37 percent in 1958 but fell to a position trailing all others with only 12 percent in 1968. In 1958 half of all these large metropolitan areas were served by at least one free-access college, but by 1968 only one-third were. Ohio, for example, had no accessible institutions in four of its five metropolitan areas of this size.

If Illinois were separated from the rest of the Midwest, the regional statistics would illustrate even less college accessibility. Instead of two-thirds of the regional population being without accessible institutions in 1958 and 1968, nearly three-fourths would have been. In 1958 three of the region's five most populous states had coverage below the national average, and in 1968 four out of five had (Table 16). During this period, Illinois, the region's most populous state, increased from 43 percent to 56 percent; and Missouri, in climbing toward the national average, doubled its coverage from 20 percent to 41 percent. Ohio, second in population, demonstrated little change as only 1 out of 8 residents lived within commuting distance of a free-access college in either 1958 or 1968. Indiana, whose population ranked fourth in the region and twelfth in the nation in 1968, ranked near the bottom in coverage for both years. In 1958 there were two institutions providing low-cost, nonselective higher education to 5 percent of the population, but by 1968 with one institution becoming too costly, the other too selective, and no new accessible colleges being established, free-access higher education in the state was unavailable.

Wisconsin, which led the nation with 86 percent coverage in 1958, dropped sharply to 47 percent a decade later. Despite this drop, however, approximately 90 percent of the blacks, most of whom live in Milwaukee, lived relatively near an accessible institution both in 1958 and 1968. No state with a major contingent of blacks can match Wisconsin's coverage for either year.

The major cities of the Midwest and the West led the nation with 44 percent coverage in 1968, and the growth within the large metropolises of the Midwest was second only to that of the Northeast. The credit for this increase and for the current high regional standing belongs primarily to those who have planned and brought to fruition the outstanding free-access college systems in Chicago and St. Louis. Almost all of Chicago's colleges are campuses of the Chicago Junior College, which dates back to 1911 and in 1968 consisted of eight campuses. The Junior College District of St. Louis county, which in-

Table 16. Percentage of different population groups within commuting distance of a free-access college, by state, 1958 and 1968 — Midwest region

	Percentage within commuting distance							
	White		Black		Puerto Rican		Total	
State	1958	1968	1958	1968	1958	1968	1958	1968
Illinois	41	56	63	59	64	57	43	56
Indiana	6	0	3	0	—	—	5	0
Iowa	25	39	14	52	—	—	25	39
Kansas	38	42	56	59	—	—	39	43
Michigan	37	41	29	33	—	—	36	40
Minnesota	19	30	4	24	—	—	19	29
Missouri	21	39	11	60	—	—	20	41
Nebraska	33	16	79	0	—	—	34	16
North Dakota	37	30	—	—	—	—	37	30
Ohio	12	12	24	19	—	—	13	12
South Dakota	23	12	—	0	—	—	22	12
Wisconsin	81	47	91	89	—	—	86	47
Regional average	30	33	35	39	64	57	31	33
National average	29	42	33	47	48	47	30	42

— Base too small for reliable estimate

cludes all the free-access colleges in St. Louis, was established only seven years ago and at present includes three campuses. Both cities have located their institutions in strategic areas, accessible to a large majority of their populations. St. Louis, for example, had 78 percent coverage of its black residents in 1968, and Chicago had 63 percent; both cities had nearly 70 percent coverage of their white residents, and Chicago had a college within commuting distance of almost 60 percent of its large Puerto Rican population. In 1958 the scene was virtually the same in Chicago but drastically different in St. Louis. At that time not one Missouri free-access college was within 50 miles of St. Louis, and the best opportunity for a commuting student with limited funds was a single low-cost but moderately selective teacher's college.

To demonstrate the extent to which the Chicago coverage has camouflaged intraregional imbalance among very large cities, one can separate the Chicago data from the remainder and discover that only 11 percent of the people living in all other major cities of the Midwest were within commuting distance of a free-access college in 1958. This contrasts with 34 percent when Chicago is included. In 1968, using the same procedure, the coverage falls from 44 percent to 30 percent. When the St. Louis figures are also taken out of the regional data in 1968, the figure is reduced to 24 percent. In other words, in the six other major cities in the Midwest, fewer than 1 out of 4 persons lived near a free-access college in 1968. Only Cincinnati provided no coverage at all.

South. Despite the fact that the South is the second fastest growing region in the nation (the West, of course, is the fastest), nearly 50 percent of its population still remains in nonmetropolitan areas. Another third live in metropolitan areas of less than one million. One would think that with such demographic characteristics it would be extremely difficult to place accessible institutions within commuting range of large numbers of people. The fact is, however, that its regional coverage is on a par with that of the more affluent and widely heralded West, and it has been accomplished by virtually the only way possible — the South has established more colleges than any other region. Not only did it have more free-access institutions in 1958, but it also created twice as many as any other region in the subsequent decade. North Carolina led the way with 24, followed by Florida with 21, and Alabama with 18. The bulk of the institutions have been either two-year technical institutes or community colleges, and their creation has not been without opposition. Often the opponents were representatives of public senior institutions, many of which were themselves free-access colleges.

Evidence of the success the South has had in increasing educational opportunity lies in the locations of the 167 new institutions. In 1958 nearly 40 percent of all the metropolitan areas were without any free-access colleges, but in 1968 less than 15 percent were. Also, undoubtedly resulting from the widely scattered population throughout the region, 3 out of 5 new colleges were established in nonmetropolitan areas and only 1 of 6 in the 16 metropolitan areas with a population of a half million or more. The product of this distribution is the highest nonmetropolitan area coverage of any region, above average coverage within intermediate metropolitan areas, and average major metropolitan area coverage. (Table 14.) It is only in the large metropolitan areas that its coverage falls below that of the West, a fact that might be partially attributable to the "spread-out" philosophy that still permeates the South. The feeling seems to exist that people are and should be spread out and that each college can and does provide opportunities for everyone living within an area of predetermined size. The question of population density often seems to be given secondary consideration. Florida, for example, has tended to emphasize a 35 mile commuting distance as a reasonable statewide working assumption. Building upon that assumption it has estimated that 99 percent of the state's population is within range of an accessible institution (State Junior College Advisory Board of Florida, 1963). Of course, this guideline has been sufficiently flexible so as to wisely allow such developments as the establishment of two campuses of Miami-Dade Junior College well within 70 or even 35 miles of each other. Only by such overlap of commuting areas can the availability of educational opportunities in large metropolitan areas approximate sufficiency.

Despite the laudable growth throughout the region, considerable state imbalances have developed. Certain states have forged ahead, often quite rapidly, while others have lagged behind. Virginia is a notable example of the former. A decade ago practically no one in the state lived near an accessible institution; by 1968, 1 out of 2 persons did. Most of the progress began in 1965 when the first of a series of technical schools and community colleges opened.

This was followed a year later by the establishment of the Virginia Community College System.

Florida, Alabama, and the Carolinas have all made unusual progress. All four states have more than doubled their coverage since 1958 (Table 17), with Florida making the largest, most widely publicized, and most intensely examined increase. Florida's rapid growth has been chronicled so often that it would be redundant to repeat it here.

In 1958 North Carolina provided free-access higher education to 1 resident in 3, primarily through public senior institutions. Since that time, however, most of these institutions have become too selective, and the state has created an uncommon balance of technical institutes and community colleges to assume the accessibility function. These latter institutions have blanketed the state to such an extent that in 1968 North Carolina ranked second only to Connecticut in coverage, with 68 percent. Despite this coverage, however, the proportion of North Carolina high school graduates who attend college is among the lowest in the nation.

South Carolina and Alabama have chosen different institutional models, but both have achieved almost identical accessibility statistics. South Carolina has established about a dozen technical education centers in all major

Table 17. Percentage of different population groups within commuting distance of a free-access college, by state, 1958 and 1968 — Southern region

| | Percentage within commuting distance | | | | | | | |
| | White | | Black | | Mexican American | | Total | |
State	1958	1968	1958	1968	1958	1968	1958	1968
Alabama	27	57	25	54	—	—	26	56
Arkansas	42	31	38	50	—	—	41	31
Delaware	19	35	24	44	—	—	19	35
Florida	25	62	32	72	—	—	27	64
Georgia	24	33	34	24	—	—	26	30
Kentucky	35	51	32	69	—	—	34	52
Louisiana	31	49	31	47	—	—	32	48
Maryland	44	59	35	47	—	—	43	57
Mississippi	73	67	75	63	—	—	74	65
North Carolina	32	69	31	67	—	—	32	68
Oklahoma	51	31	47	26	—	—	51	31
South Carolina	26	58	21	53	—	—	24	56
Tennessee	34	39	46	52	—	—	36	41
Texas	48	37	53	43	60	40	50	38
Virginia	2	52	3	40	—	—	2	50
West Virginia	46	53	50	59	—	—	46	54
Regional average	35	50	36	52	60	40	36	50
National average	29	42	33	47	48	47	30	42

— Base too small for reliable estimate

cities and throughout most of the populous areas of the state since 1958. In so doing it has raised its coverage from a below-average 24 percent to a well-above-average 56 percent. During the same period Alabama has created more than a dozen state-sponsored junior colleges and has also succeeded in covering all its major cities and most of its populous counties.

While nearly all its neighbors have demonstrated sharp increases in the past decade, Georgia has made very slow progress. At the same time that it established a half-dozen new two-year institutions, several of its public four-year colleges were climbing to higher levels of inaccessibility, thereby resulting in only a very modest gain (26 percent to 30 percent).

The situation in Oklahoma is even more critical. Not only have no free-access colleges been established since 1958, but no public two-year institutions of any kind have been organized since 1919. Furthermore, Oklahoma State University and the University of Oklahoma, both free-access institutions a decade ago, are currently too selective in the applicants they actually admit. Several other state four-year colleges have followed the same route, and between 1958 and 1968 accessibility coverage dropped from 51 percent to 31 percent.

Texas, too, lost ground during the sixties. Although it did add several community colleges, its population increased and became urbanized to such an extent that coverage dropped from 50 percent to 38 percent. Evidently realizing that things were not as they should or could be, the state legislature took steps in 1965 to organize the development of higher education rather than leave it subject to the whims of local areas. While there has been a great deal of talk and while appropriations have increased modestly since then, Texas has yet to exercise aggressive leadership in this vital area.

Just as some Southern states have increased and others have decreased their coverage between 1958 and 1968, so also have the largest cities of the South. Miami stands as a widely known success story in that its dual-campus Miami-Dade Junior College has had the effect of bringing almost total (94 percent) coverage to a city that a decade earlier had no accessible institution to offer its residents. New Orleans also had no coverage in 1958, but within 10 years, through the establishment of a public two-year college and a branch of the state university, it had provided coverage for more than 4 of 10 residents. Washington, D. C., also increased its coverage dramatically, chiefly through the creation of Federal City College and Washington Technical Institute. By 1968 the city was able to offer an accessible college to more than 80 percent of its residents, the majority of whom were black. The student demand on these institutions, however, was so great in 1968 that literally thousands of applicants were turned away.

Unfortunately, the story of cities that moved in the opposite direction also exists and must be told. Atlanta and Houston, for example, both dropped from nearly complete coverage in 1958 to a position where only 1 resident in 8 was within commuting distance of a free-access college in 1968. Both are among the fastest growing cities in the South, and this factor was directly responsible for Houston's decrease. In 1958 there was one free-access college in Houston, but the city was small enough for almost everyone to live within commuting distance of it. Ten years later, however, the city had physically grown away from the institution, and no other had been built to take up the slack.

Atlanta's situation was somewhat different, for not only did the city grow away from the one college that existed as free-access in 1958, but at the same time that institution became too selective. Its 1968 freshman class was comprised almost entirely of students who had graduated from the top half of their high school classes. Like Houston, no institution was developed in Atlanta to fill the gap, although in both cities one such institution was established in the suburbs.

The Houston situation illustrates a subtle problem that can easily be camouflaged among data such as that generated by this study. The problem is one of racial imbalance, and it has been referred to on various occasions throughout this report. It must be mentioned again at this time so as to reemphasize the importance of treating coverage figures within the Southern states with a measure of caution. The lone free-access institution in Houston is Texas Southern University (TSU) with an enrollment that is 99 percent black. To say that all the city's whites who live within commuting distance of TSU have free access to higher education is to oversimplify or even idealize away the very real problem. Because of tradition and social taboos, almost no white person living there would consider himself to live in proximity to an accessible institution.

West. Eyes have traditionally turned westward at the mention of free-access or open-door higher education, and rightfully so. For years California has had the largest community college operation in the country; in fact, it had more public two-year colleges 20 years ago than any other state had two years ago. The California influence on its two northern neighbors, Oregon and Washington, evidently has a long history, for in 1958 the three were far ahead of the other Western states as each provided an accessible college to roughly 1 of every 2 residents. (Table 18.)

As indicated in Table 14, the primary increase in coverage in the West occurred among metropolitan areas of less than one million. Areas from one-half to one million experienced the most vigorous growth as they moved from 40 percent to 55 percent coverage. There was practically no change in the accessibility of either the very large metropolitan areas or the nonmetropolitan counties.

The situation in nonmetropolitan areas appears somewhat anomalous at first glance. Consider three circumstances that developed in these areas between 1958 and 1968: (1) the population actually decreased, (2) 45 percent of the 86 new free-access colleges in the West were established there, and (3) there was only a slight positive change in their coverage. One would logically assume that when such an influx of institutions is accompanied by a decrease in population (no matter how slight), there would be a significant increase in the percentage of the remaining population within commuting distance of these institutions. Since this is not the case, an explanation is in order. Three

Table 18. Percentage of different population groups within commuting distance of a free-access college, by state, 1958 and 1968 — Western region

| | *Percentage within commuting distance* | | | | | | | |
| | *White* | | *Black* | | *Mexican American* | | *Total* | |
State	*1958*	*1968*	*1958*	*1968*	*1958*	*1968*	*1958*	*1968*
Alaska	27	31	—	50	—	—	27	31
Arizona	35	37	39	42	30	30	34	38
California	53	60	57	48	57	66	54	60
Colorado.	19	41	10	58	40	48	21	42
Hawaii.	0	48	—	60	—	—	0	48
Idaho	36	40	—	0	—	—	36	40
Montana	30	31	—	0	—	—	30	31
Nevada	28	0	—	0	—	—	27	0
New Mexico	14	24	17	38	19	16	16	22
Oregon	45	49	70	75	—	—	45	49
Utah.	28	19	—	67	—	—	28	20
Washington.	45	51	45	53	—	—	45	51
Wyoming.	30	43	—	50	—	—	30	43
Regional average	43	51	52	48	45	55	44	51
National average	29	42	33	47	48	47	30	42

— Base too small for reliable estimate

possibilities exist. The new colleges could have been placed in counties that already were moderately well covered by an existing institution, they could have been placed in sparsely populated areas of even the populous counties, or several institutions that existed as free-access colleges in 1958 could have either closed or become too costly and/or too selective, thereby forcing the new colleges to take up the slack. What actually occurred was a combination of the second and third possibilities. Almost all the colleges were located in sparsely populated areas and together covered a very small proportion of the region's residents, but they were also forced to make up for the loss of 27 institutions accessible in 1958 but not a decade later. Only a few of the new colleges had commuting areas that even partially overlapped those of existing colleges.

The lack of increase in coverage within the major metropolitan areas is largely attributable to the phenomenal population growth these areas have experienced. They increased by nearly 40 percent in the sixties after already doubling in the fifties. Currently more than half the region's population resides in these areas of more than one million people. The colleges that were established in the past decade have grown significantly but have only been able to keep pace with the burgeoning population.

The West, and particularly California, has been particularly active in providing accessible higher education to residents of the fringes of these major areas in recent years. But in so doing many areas of the large central cities have been neglected. Of the 30 new colleges established in California between 1958 and 1968, only five were in central cities while 13 were in fringe areas. Many reasonable arguments could be set forth supporting this development, not the least of which might be the availability and cost of land. The fact remains, however, that where two-thirds of all fringe residents lived within commuting distance of an accessible institution in 1968, less than half of those living in the central cities did. The situation in Los Angeles is illustrative. Although a fringe resident of Los Angeles had approximately a 26 percent better chance of living near a free-access college than did his city counterpart in 1958, only one of the several new colleges developed in the metropolitan area between 1958 and 1968 was placed within the Los Angeles city limits. In addition, the changing character and increasing urbanization of the city has created a more favorable accessibility situation for the white and Mexican American city dwellers, but a less favorable one for the black residents. Although the coverage increased about 5 percent for whites and Mexican Americans between 1958 and 1968, it plummeted from 61 percent down to 26 percent for blacks. (It should be pointed out that more Mexican Americans live in the fringe areas than in the city itself, and almost all of them were within commuting distance of a free-access institution in 1968.)

Lest one think that Los Angeles is an isolated case, the statistics for San Francisco, San Diego, and Seattle are similar. For years the only free-access college in San Francisco has been its City College, and between 1958 and 1968 the proportion of the city's residents who lived within commuting distance of this institution dropped from 47 percent to 37 percent, affecting each racial group alike. At the same time, however, the fringe areas were recipients of several new colleges with coverage rising from 44 percent to 68 percent.

Despite the addition of Mesa College (in a predominantly white area), San Diego's city coverage dropped from 50 percent to 31 percent while its fringe coverage moved in the opposite direction. Seattle suffered an even greater loss as its city coverage tumbled from 86 percent to 32 percent. In 1958 the University of Washington provided almost total coverage, but in subsequent years the city has grown and the university has become fairly selective. Fortunately, Seattle Community College was created and has provided educational opportunity for a portion of the city's residents, but two-thirds remained without coverage in 1968. During this same period, the fringe area moved from 0 percent to 57 percent coverage.

While one can certainly appreciate and applaud the positive steps taken in these fringe areas, one might at the same time hope that the insufficient attention paid so many major cities will soon be corrected. The problems of urban areas such as San Francisco, Los Angeles, Seattle, Atlanta, and Boston are definitely not going to become less complex and less troublesome by creating accessible higher education in the suburbs while letting major cities smolder in their status quo.

Denver is a good example of a city that recently has taken a hard look at its educational deficiencies and, like St. Louis, has done something about them. Within the past five years it has established both a public four-year college and a multicampus community college. In so doing it has raised its coverage from 0 percent in 1958 to nearly 50 percent of all Denver residents in 1968. Slightly more than half of the city's black and Mexican American populations reside within commuting distance of one of the institutions. This increase in Colorado's largest city also accounts in large measure for the doubling of the state's coverage (from 21 percent to 42 percent).

Other states that have made noteworthy progress include Hawaii and Wyoming. In 1965 Hawaii developed a community college system affiliated with the state university, and since that date it has placed six campuses throughout the islands, thereby increasing its population coverage from 0 percent to 48 percent.

Wyoming is exceptional because it is the only state to have nothing but public free-access institutions in both 1958 and 1968. Because one new community college was established in 1959 in the southwestern portion of the state, coverage rose from 30 percent to 43 percent.

In summary, the West is irrevocably influenced by activities in California, where about 1 out of 2 Westerners live. The expectations that have been raised in that state by the promise of free-access higher education to all are reflected in activity in other states. The community college model is widely used, although each state has asserted its sovereignty by devising a unique plan. All but two states, Nevada and Utah, increased their coverage over the decade, but as is to be expected from states involved in this movement for a comparatively long period of time, progress has been more moderate than in the South (which is trying to catch up) or in the Northeast (which is beginning to wake up).

The large cities of the West are the current trouble spot. In recent years attention has tended to focus on the fringe areas, despite the mounting inaccessibility of educational opportunities in several cities. The problem is not easy to solve, given the unavailability and high cost of land, particularly in California, and the lack of political "sex appeal" that accompanies involvement in urban crises. It is, however, one that must be dealt with if the West intends to continue providing leadership to the rest of the nation in matters of college accessibility.

4. The components of change in free-access higher education

The present character of free-access higher education is the result of the operation of many forces. Within the past decade automation and the changing technology have forced higher education to take on new functions; new population configurations, maturation of the postwar babies, and an increased proportion of high school graduates have necessitated new institutions; new levels of federal, state, and local support have permitted this necessity to become a reality; master plans have come into vogue in an attempt to organize the growth of both free- and non-free-access higher education so that the educational needs of all citizens can be met. The list could go on.

Up to this point this study has focused on a description of the nature of free-access higher education development. In this chapter, however, attention is placed on several factors that seem to have had a direct effect, both positively and negatively, on this growth. The factors to be discussed include construction of new institutions, urbanization, college relocation, increased tuition, increased selectivity, and college closings.

New institutions

Perhaps the most striking fact about the growth of higher education in the past 10 years is that new free-access colleges have been established in large numbers and in practically every state; 390 new colleges were created, an average of slightly under one a week. In addition, 28 institutions moderately inaccessible in 1958 became free-access by 1968. (Eleven of the 28 were in New York state and had 1958 tuition charges just a few dollars above the free-access limit of $230.) In total there were 418 new free-access colleges.

As most lay observers and professional educators well understand, the kind of institution largely responsible for this boom has been the community college. Of the 390 new colleges, 367 were public two-year institutions. Only four were private, with most of the remainder being branch campuses of state universities.

An equally well-known fact is that California led the rest of the country, having established 30 new community colleges. New York ranked second with 28 institutions, followed by Illinois and North Carolina with 26 each. Only five states — Indiana, Maine, Nevada, Oklahoma, and South Dakota — failed to establish at least one. Nationally they were located in such a manner as to extend low-cost, nonselective educational opportunities to one quarter of the population not already served by an existing college. (Table 19.) It would be incorrect to say that opportunity was given to 25 percent who had not had it in 1958, for as shall be indicated later, some of these 418 colleges were placed in areas previously served by an institution that during the decade became inaccessible.

Groups reaping the greatest opportunity benefit from the establishment of new colleges were Puerto Ricans living in New York City (36 percent) and blacks living throughout the Northeast (34 percent). On the other hand, those profiting least were Mexican Americans (14 percent in the West and 16 percent in the South) and whites in the Midwest (16 percent).

The region making the largest gain was the Northeast, a not unexpected consequence since that area had such a small percentage of coverage in 1958 and had large population concentrations conspicuous by their lack of educational opportunity. The compactness of the region as a whole and the tendency of the majority of the population to cluster in several geographically small metropolitan areas have made it possible to cover large numbers of people with comparatively few colleges. The New York City situation is notable in this regard and, although mentioned in the last chapter, bears reemphasis. In 1958 not one free-access college was located in either the central city or the fringe areas, which together contained about 10 million people (nearly one-fourth of the region's total population), but by 1968 five institutions had been established throughout the city alone, with another four in the suburban fringe. This development put free-access higher education within reach of approximately 30 percent of the population in each area. Among minority groups Puerto Ricans fared better than the city average (36 percent); blacks were considerably below average (21 percent). Even as of this writing no free-access college has been located in Harlem, one of the most densely populated areas of the country.[1]

Table 19. Percentage of different population groups within commuting distance of new† free-access colleges, by region, 1968

| Region | Number of new colleges | Percentage within commuting distance | | | |
		White	Black	Brown*	Total
Northeast	79	32	34	36	32
Midwest	86	16	17	26	16
South	167	29	29	16	29
West	86	20	20	14	19
United States	418	24	27	18	25

† Includes 28 colleges that were non-free-access colleges in 1958.
* Mexican Americans in five southwestern states and Puerto Ricans in New York City and Chicago.

Based on the data presented in the two preceding chapters, one might have anticipated the comparatively small increase in the Midwest and West. Although both regions established more new colleges than the Northeast did, expanded coverage was hampered for various reasons. One was that there were no situations like New York City, whereby a few strategically located in-

1. Several writers on the urban crisis have noted that if we all lived as crushed together as the blacks and others in Harlem, the total population of the United States would be squeezed into three of the five boroughs of New York City.

stitutions could skyrocket the amount of coverage. St. Louis came the closest, and its development did have a strong effect on the Midwest totals.

Another reason for only modest growth in the Midwest is that the region covers a large territory, and pockets of population have developed around seemingly every grain elevator. (A similar phenomenon has occurred in several parts of the South.) One of the several effects of this settlement pattern has been that political power tends to be diffuse, and interested parties lobby for higher educational representation in their respective areas. The success of these groups coupled with the widespread belief that public colleges ought to be geographically spread out has resulted in a host of colleges serving comparatively small populations. Both the Midwest and the South established a majority of their colleges in areas with populations under 250,000, but the Midwest did so while having less than half its population in these areas whereas the South had more than half.

The problem in the West is different. Although it has twice as much land area as the second largest region, the South, its population is highly urbanized with approximately one-half living in the seven major metropolitan areas. California, with five of these areas, is the fastest growing state in the country, and the 30 institutions it established between 1958 and 1968 were barely enough to keep it ahead of the population surge. With the population of the major central cities filled to overflowing, city dwellers and those moving into the state have headed for fringe areas in unprecedented numbers. Given this demographic characteristic, it is understandable that almost half the new colleges were located in the fringe.

Through a concentrated program of need assessment and college construction, the South established almost twice as many colleges as any other region (167) and placed them within reach of 29 percent of its population. Even when the population distribution of the region is taken into account, the smaller metropolitan areas and nonmetropolitan counties received more than their share of institutions.

Analyzing the placement of new free-access colleges according to community size, it is readily apparent that inequities exist. For example, although major metropolitan areas contain more than one-third of the nation's people, they have received less than one-fourth of all new institutions established since 1958. In fact about the same number of new colleges were built in nonmetropolitan areas as in all metropolitan areas. Metropolitan areas, however, hold almost twice as many people (66 percent to 34 percent).

The resources available to various institutions is a factor that must be considered when comparing the accessibility of colleges in one region or community with those in another. Neither the South nor the Northeast, for instance, have supported their free-access colleges to the extent that the other two regions traditionally have. Since resources are directly translated into space, buildings, and programs which in turn make it possible to serve a given number of students in particular ways, one must be careful lest the growth that has taken place in these two regions be viewed overenthusiastically. In the South the problem continues to rest primarily with a lack of state financial resources (with a few exceptions), whereas in the Northeast it is more a matter of inadequate appropriations. The wealth is there, but thus far the giving is not.

Urbanization

Discussion of the "urban crisis" has become so frequent in recent years that it is rapidly losing its poignancy. Statistics stating that 7 out of every 10 Americans live in cities that occupy only 1 percent of this country's total land area no longer surprise many in this age of ecological and social awareness. Nevertheless, such statistics must be stated because they are real and because the problems caused by such concentrations of population in some way affect the lives of the vast majority of people in the nation. Unemployment, underemployment, inadequate housing, gross poverty, lack of educational opportunities, and social disorganization are facts of life for a growing number of city dwellers.

It is not the purpose of this section of this study to present a far-reaching discussion of the totality of problems endemic in urban life but rather to focus on one: the effect increased urbanization has had on the accessibility of low-cost, nonselective collegiate institutions in the decade 1958-1968. Others have performed the former task, many with both power and eloquence, but their voices are slow to be heard. Of the many excellent works available today, two which need to be read, understood, and acted upon are Kenneth Clark's *Dark Ghetto* and the *Report of the National Advisory Commission on Civil Disorders*. Although differing in approach, their analyses of the problems of city residents in general, and black city residents in particular, are compelling.

The rather simplistic test for the effect of urbanization employed in this study is based on the assumption that the geographic accessibility of an educational institution is affected either by its movement with respect to the population or the population's movement with respect to it. While college relocation will be treated in the following section, population movement will be discussed at this time. Only colleges that were free-access and in the same location in both 1958 and 1968 (to be called Type A colleges), have been used in making this analysis.

While increased urbanization may bring only negative consequences to many aspects of life, it theoretically can have either a positive or negative effect on the accessibility of higher education. If the population near an institution increases to a greater extent than it does elsewhere, the effect will be positive, as both more people and a greater proportion of the area's population will be within commuting distance. If, however, the city grows away from the college (as in the Houston case discussed in the previous chapter), the proportion of the population located near this institution will decrease. This phenomenon could occur even as the amount of coverage increases. For example, a college located in an old section of town may increase its absolute coverage as the area experiences moderate growth, possibly through urban renewal or model cities programs, but may actually undergo a loss in percentage of coverage because newer portions of the city are growing at a more rapid rate.

As the typical metropolitan area grows, mobility tends to become restricted. Not only is it more difficult to move from place to place, but the "other side of town" also takes on a foreboding quality that seems to be directly proportional to travel time. Attendance at a college five or ten miles away may have been quite feasible when it took only 15 to 20 minutes to commute, but it lies beyond the distance many potential students are willing to journey if 45 to 60 minutes are required. Not only would such an ordeal take up to two hours of their time each day, but they would also be required to leave familiar neighborhoods where they are known, to travel to areas in which they may feel both unknown and unwanted.

When one looks at either national or regional data (Table 20), urbanization does not immediately appear to have had a large affect on college accessibility. For example, where 19 percent of the total national population was within commuting distance of this category of free-access institutions in 1958, the figure had dropped to 17 percent by 1968. Although this represents a loss of more than three million people, it does not bring to light the nature of the problems involved.

With reference to Table 20, the lack of any apparent change in the Northeast is a result more of the absence of free-access institutions, particularly in the major cities, than of the lack of population migration. In fact there were no free-access institutions that met the previously stated criteria in any of the major metropolitan areas of the Northeast. The West, on the other hand, accounted for three-fifths of all colleges located in these areas, with all but two located in California.

Since increased urbanization has a more critical effect on inhabitants of large cities, this section of the study will concentrate on metropolitan areas of 500,000 or more. The extent to which these areas have been affected is demonstrated by the fact that although the number of residents increased 44 percent in the past decade, the coverage by Type A colleges increased only 30 percent. Had there been no affect of urbanization, one should have expected the coverage to have kept pace with the population surge and also to have risen 44 percent.

Although one cannot generalize from a few examples, it may be helpful to an understanding of the urbanization factor to briefly describe the situations in six metropolitan areas—Baltimore, Chicago, Kansas City, Los Angeles, Memphis, and San Francisco-Oakland. The reasons for this particular selection are: (1) these areas represent various sections of the country, (2) they vary in population size and demographic characteristics, (3) each has more than one free-access institution that has been in the same location since 1958, and (4) they demonstrate assorted outcomes.

Baltimore is typical of major metropolitan areas in having undergone a significant population rise in its fringe areas since 1958 while at the same time suffering a small loss in the number residing within the central city. The word

Table 20. Percentage of the population within commuting distance of Type A free-access colleges, by region, 1958 and 1968

Region	Number of institutions	Percentage within commuting distance 1958	Percentage within commuting distance 1968
Northeast	13	6	6
Midwest	102	18	16
South	143	25	21
West	103	33	31
United States	361	19	17

"suffering" is appropriate because, like so many metropolises, the trend is toward racial and economic segregation of the central city. Middle-income families, predominantly white, have been moving out, and low-income families, predominantly black, have been moving in. Between 1958 and 1968 there was virtually no change in the extent to which Type A colleges covered the total Baltimore metropolitan area. There was, however, a marked difference in the central city as the 18 percent coverage in 1958 was reduced by one-third a decade later. Although the population of the fringe areas had doubled during the period, Type A colleges were distributed on three sides of the city, thus being able to absorb this influx with only a slight loss in coverage percentage.

Chicago experienced a similar shift in population over the 10-year period, but its Type A college distribution was such that it had exactly the opposite effect. Where Baltimore had only one Type A college in its central city, Chicago had several located throughout the city. They particularly covered the pockets of black population so that as the white exodus continued, the central city coverage increased from 42 percent to 55 percent. The fringe areas, on the other hand, were unprepared for this movement, which tended to spread in all directions, and the single college in Joliet was able to cover only one-tenth of this inflated population; 10 years earlier it had provided accessible higher education to more than one-fifth. Fortunately, several new colleges were established in other suburbs so that by 1968 Chicago's fringe coverage had actually increased rather than decreased.

Kansas City is an example of a metropolitan area that has grown both in its twin central cities and in its outlying areas. The proportion of the population covered by Type A colleges in the Kansas City area dropped from 32 percent to 22 percent. The fringe areas, slightly covered in 1958, were left completely uncovered 10 years later. A small decrease of whites in the central cities was more than offset by the immigration of blacks. The blacks evidently settled near one of the colleges, for the proportion of black coverage rose from 45 percent to 55 percent.

The Los Angeles area just seems to keep growing. Its 16 Type A colleges have been distributed so widely throughout the area that regardless of the location of the growth, it has been largely covered by one of these institutions. Because the increased land area of the fringe has made it more difficult to cover, there was a slight drop in fringe coverage in 1968; nevertheless, it remained above 60 percent for both years. City coverage, which included Long Beach, was stable at 40 percent. All was not well, however, for as various population groups shifted among neighborhoods and were joined by others from outside the area, the nature of coverage changed. White coverage in the central cities showed a slight increase between 1958 and 1968, Mexican American coverage stayed about the same, but black coverage dropped sharply. Where more than half the blacks lived near a Type A college in 1958, less than one-fifth did in 1968. The data show that the actual number of blacks dropped by more than one-third; giving rise to the explanation that many blacks covered by a Type A college in 1958 moved to a neighborhood not accessible to such an institution 10 years later. This group apparently was augmented by thousands of blacks moving into the uncovered areas during the decade.

Memphis, the smallest of the six areas discussed in this section, illustrates some of the urbanization problems of intermediate metropolitan areas evolving into large areas. Both its city and fringe areas have grown to such an extent that coverage by Type A colleges dropped from 85 percent in 1958 to 49 percent a decade later. Where its two colleges covered the entire city in 1958, it dropped to only two-thirds coverage in 1968. Blacks, who make up about 40 percent of the city's population, suffered this decrease to the same extent as whites. Fringe residents were affected as well, for practically all of the 16 percent within commuting distance of the two institutions in 1958 were beyond their range by 1968.

The San Francisco-Oakland metropolitan area, with its three million residents, has not been affected by urbanization as defined here to the extent one might suppose. One reason is that Oakland, a rapidly growing city, lacked a Type A college, and hence the affect its growth may have had on the accessibility of higher education cannot be directly demonstrated. Another reason is that Type A colleges have been strategically located throughout the Bay Area and have managed to maintain a coverage rate of one-third, despite the huge immigration that has occurred. The city of San Francisco itself, surrounded on three sides by water and on the fourth by a small mountain, is severely limited in its possibility for geographic expansion. As in many other cities, therefore, a large number of residents, particularly white, have fled to the suburbs. Many of them appear to have come from within commuting distance of the one Type A college, because the white coverage dropped from 45 percent in 1958 to 30 percent in 1968. It is feasible to suppose that a number of blacks moved into these vacated areas, because both the absolute and the percentage coverage increased between the two years. The drop in Mexican American coverage despite increased population raises the possibility that this group engaged in neighborhood shifting.

Several tentative conclusions seem evident from the regional and sample metropolitan areas. In general, urbanization has affected college accessibility, although the magnitude of that affect in this study is subject to the arbitrary distinction between population categories. In some instances the abrupt change in commuting radius brought about by this division may have resulted in an overstatement of the affect, whereas in other instances where no radius change occurred an understatement may have resulted. (This is only one reason why it is impossible to reflect local circumstances accurately through data gathered for a national study. The percentages reported for these six metropolitan areas, therefore, should be regarded only as providing examples of the kinds of affects urbanization can have in areas of varied demographic characteristics.)

As one would expect, central cities with only one or two Type A institutions have been hit harder by the movement of people than those with several, although the latter have been subject to changes in ethnic coverage even when their overall percentages remained stable. Fringe areas with a number of institutions sprinkled throughout seem to have been able to absorb the influx in population with little loss in coverage. Those with few institutions were overwhelmed by the migration.

Although the procedures employed here were necessarily straightforward and made no attempt to consider the many subtle implications of urbanization, one definite conclusion is that as areas grow, the accessibility effect of most institutions is diminished. This often occurs even though absolute coverage increases.

College relocation

Closely related to urbanization is the issue of college relocation. In the previous section of this study the discussion focused on the movement of people; in this section it focuses on the movement of colleges. As cities have grown and space has become limited, some institutions have restricted enrollments, some have bought and razed surrounding buildings, others have acquired old factories and turned them into classrooms and laboratories, while several have looked for greener pastures in less congested areas. Not a few have left facilities shared with local high schools to establish permanent campuses of their own.

Although a host of free-access colleges, particularly community colleges, have moved into new quarters within the past few years, only 10 meet the criteria established for college relocation in this study, and these are classified as Type B colleges.[2] Most of the others did not qualify either because they were established following 1958 and, therefore, classified as new institutions or because their relocation consisted of a change within a city other than a central city of a large metropolitan area. An example of the first type of disqualification is Forest Park Community College in St. Louis, which first offered classes in 1963 in high school facilities, but which moved to its new permanent

2. The criteria were: (1) an institution had to exist as a free-access college in both 1958 and 1968, and (2) it had to move from one city to another during this period, unless it was located in the central city of a large metropolitan area (500,000 or more) in which case any address change was acceptable.

campus in 1967. An example of the second is the College of San Mateo (CSM), located about 15 miles south of San Francisco. Although it moved in 1963 to a picturesque new campus in the hills, it remained within the city limits of San Mateo. The relocation of colleges like Forest Park and CSM has undoubtedly had an affect on their accessibility to community residents, but the nature or extent of this affect cannot be calculated from the data available. The only statement that seems warranted is that when colleges move from temporary downtown facilities, they tend to migrate toward suburban areas where land is both less expensive and more plentiful. Such a move, however, may reduce the city coverage while raising the suburban coverage, a situation that does not seem completely justifiable when one considers that the average family income of city dwellers in major metropolitan areas is 25 percent lower than the average family income of those on the fringe (United States Bureau of the Census, 1969).

The 10 Type B colleges represent practically every community type from the central city and fringe areas of very large metropolitan areas to rural counties. All were public two-year institutions, and seven of the 10 relocated in the same county. Taken together they covered 33 percent fewer people in 1968 than they did in 1958, a drop attributed to urbanization, to the new commuting areas that in some cases overlapped those of existing free-access colleges, and to the fact that in other cases the institutions simply moved into less congested areas. Blacks, whites, and browns all lost coverage.

Increased tuition

Anyone interested in higher education has been aware that student educational costs have been rising rapidly over the past decade. By and large, however, these increases seem to have occurred in the private sector where the average tuition charge went from $550 in 1958 to $1,170 in 1968. Public charges during the same period rose from $145 to $225. Although tuition and fees at free-access institutions did increase during the decade (the average went from $110 to $220), the gain was generally proportional to the rise in family income. In other words, it cost the typical family roughly the same proportion of its income to send a child to a free-access college in 1968 as it had in 1958.

Rising costs alone, then, did not appear to be a major factor in the removal of 1958 free-access institutions from the 1968 roster. Only 18 colleges that continued to be nonselective in the latter year had raised their tuition and fees above the $400 limit, with half of them charging between $400 and $500. The number of people left uncovered by this move toward inaccessibility was less than two million, and the population most affected were white residents of Southern nonmetropolitan areas.

Increased selectivity

Although increased costs appeared to have only a negligible effect on college accessibility, increased selectivity was of major importance. Institutions, particularly state colleges and universities whose operations had been traditionally guided by the open-admissions principle, found themselves overwhelmed by the crush of students during the sixties. While virtually all responded by increasing their enrollments, a large number also raised academic standards. This latter action was undoubtedly dictated by at least three factors working in concert. First, resources for capital and educational improvements were limited; second, many in the academic community, including faculty and students, felt that quality education suffered when enrollments became too large; and third, community colleges were developing and were willing to work with the less academically prepared students.

The rise in selectivity, and hence, in inaccessibility, was pervasive enough to cause 20 percent of all 1958 free-access institutions to have left these ranks 10 years later. Of the 109 colleges in this group, 88 were either state colleges or universities. A large portion continued to maintain the outward appearance (low tuition) of accessibility in 1968, but at the same time they limited enrollment almost exclusively to graduates from the top half of their high school class. In some cases the stated admissions policy still bespeaks broad accessibility, while the credentials of the entering class suggest at least moderate selectivity.

Three-fourths of these once-free-access-now-selective colleges are located in the South and Midwest, with the majority in each region situated in either small metropolitan areas or nonmetropolitan counties. Although the West had only 16 institutions in this category, nine were state universities — a fact that is not surprising in light of the community college growth in the region. The universities evidently felt themselves freed from the obligation to provide for the below-average student who might desire a college education. The Northeast lost the fewest free-access institutions because of selectivity, but then again the Northeast had the fewest to lose. The fact that not one state university in this region became too selective between 1958 and 1968 should not bring joy to the advocate of universal access to higher education, because the main campus of every state university had already become too selective *prior* to 1958.

As indicated in Table 21, of the four methods by which an institution could become non-free-access, increased selectivity affected a larger proportion of the population than all others combined. The South and Midwest, each with 7 percent coverage in 1958, contributed the most to this loss. Despite the fact that most colleges in all regions were in nonmetropolitan areas, those hardest hit were the whites and blacks in large metropolitan areas and Mexican Americans in small metropolitan areas.

There was also a handful (12) of institutions that became both too costly and too selective during the decade. Like those that were only too selective, they tended to be state colleges and universities, with three-fourths located in the South and Midwest. Their combined coverage in 1958 consisted of less than one million people so that their affect on national accessibility of higher education is minimal.

College closings

While some institutions no longer serve a free-access function because they have chosen to raise costs or entrance requirements, another group has simply ceased to exist.[3] There were 28 institutions in this category, with the large majority publicly controlled.

Table 21. Percentage within commuting distance of 1958 free-access colleges which were not free-access in 1968, by disqualification type and by region, 1958

Disqualification type	Number of colleges	Percentage within commuting distance				
		NE	MW	S	W	U.S.
Costs too high	18	0	1	2	2	1
Selectivity too high	109	4	7	7	5	6
Costs and selectivity too high	12	0	1	0	0	1
Closed[a]	28	4	2	1	2	2
Total	167	8	11	10	9	10

a. Not listed in *Opening Fall Enrollment* in 1968

In 1958 these colleges covered 3.5 million people. Although once again three-fourths of the institutions were in the South and Midwest, almost half of the people covered were in the Northeast. In fact more than 25 percent of all the coverage provided by free-access colleges in the Northeast that year came from the four institutions that have subsequently ceased to exist.

The reasons for an institution's closing are no doubt complex, but at least two appear prominent among these 28 colleges. Some suffered from lack of students, which was also most likely tied to lack of funds, while others closed in order to merge with nearby and normally healthier institutions. Two of the South's nine Negro colleges that closed during this period merged with some of Florida's integrated community colleges.[4]

The composite picture

The construction of new institutions, urbanization, college relocation, increased costs, increased selectivity, and college closings have all had an impact on efforts to expand educational opportunity by means of free-access higher education. While it may have been useful to discuss each factor apart from the rest, it is more important for those who would plan for the future to see the importance of each in relation to the others. They must have understanding

---

3. "Existence" was operationally defined as inclusion in the 1968 *Opening Fall Enrollment*, prepared by the U.S. Office of Education. Failure to be included there may be because of an institution's closing or its inability to meet certain criteria.

4. Ten other Florida Negro colleges merged with integrated community colleges between 1962 and 1965, but they are not included in this study since they were not listed in the 1958 *Opening Fall Enrollment* and hence not considered to be in existence in the earlier year.

of those factors that have been significant in either expanding or restricting opportunity as well as those that have not been demonstrated to be of particular consequence.

Based on the data already presented in this chapter, the six factors can be placed in three categories according to their direction of impact on expanded opportunity. First, new institutions obviously have had a positive impact since they did not exist in 1958. Second, increased costs, increased selectivity, and college closings have also obviously had a negative impact since such institutions were readily accessible in 1958 but not in 1968. The third category, urbanization and college relocation, represents situations that could have either a positive or negative impact. In cases where a larger proportion of an area's residents were brought into proximity to an institution, the impact was positive; where the reverse was true, the impact was negative.

In the previous chapter emphasis was placed on the net effect of these positive and negative factors, and the data were examples of the results of change. When one knows that population coverage in the United States increased from 30 percent in 1958 to 42 percent in 1968, one knows the result of change but does not have an indication of the components that produced it. In this section these components are discussed.

Table 22 indicates that on the national level new institutions provided educational opportunity to 25 percent of the population, thereby nearly doubling the 1958 coverage. Had the demographic and college accessibility scene remained static between 1958 and 1968, approximately 55 percent of the population of the United States would have been within commuting distance of a free-access institution in 1968. This, of course, was not what transpired. Rather, people moved to new locations, colleges moved to higher levels of inaccessibility, some institutions even moved to new communities, while others either merged or closed. The net effect of all this action was that more than half the new institutional gain was eroded. The most damaging was the 6 percent loss in coverage produced by colleges becoming too selective. Urbanization, increased costs, and college closings each accounted for an additional 2 percent, while college relocation resulted in a 1 percent drop.

In order to facilitate an understanding of the impact of the new institution (or positive) factor when compared with the other primarily negative factors, a measure called Coverage Quotient (CQ) has been devised. Its purpose is to place the various factors in perspective with respect to the changed conditions of population coverage that occurred between 1958 and 1968. In short, it demonstrates the extent to which negative factors have eroded the increased coverage afforded by new colleges. It operates according to the following formula:

$$CQ = \frac{\text{the sum of the net effect (\%) of all 6 factors}}{\text{1968 coverage of new institutions (\%)}}$$

Under static conditions or under conditions where factors other than new colleges have no affect, the quotient is +1.00 The further the CQ deviates from +1.00 in the negative direction, the greater the impact of negative factors. It is

Table 22. Changes in percentage of total U.S. population within commuting distance of a free-access college according to accessibility factors, 1958 and 1968

Accessibility factors	Percentage within commuting distance		
	1958	*1968*	*Net effect*
New institutions	—	25	+25
Urbanization	19	17	− 2
College relocation	1	0	− 1
Increased costs[a]	2	—	− 2
Increased selectivity[a]	6	—	− 6
College closings	2	—	− 2
Total	30	42	+12

Coverage Quotient = +0.48

_____

a. Colleges that became both costly and selective were placed in the most appropriate category.

not only possible for the quotient to be a negative number, but it is also possible for it to exceed +1.00 provided that urbanization and/or college relocation act as positive factors.

If one applies the formula to the data in Table 22, the Coverage Quotient for the nation is +0.48. This indicates that when all factors are taken into con-

$$CQ = \frac{(+25) + (-2) + (-1) + (-2) + (-6) + (-2)}{25} = \frac{12}{25} = +0.48$$

sideration, the increase in coverage in the United States was just under one-half of what it would have been had 1958 conditions prevailed while new colleges were developed. This means that an additional 20 to 25 million people would have had a low-cost, nonselective institution accessible to them had various negative factors not been at work. (Often it appears that many who are responsible for state- or system-wide institutional development are not fully cognizant of the myriad factors and forces that do tend to restrict the accessibility of colleges to students. The factors discussed here, of course, afford only a partial look at the problem. One must also remember that college construction takes time, and during that time conditions change. Needs analyses that do not use thoughtful estimates and projections and that are not subject to frequent revision are inadequate at best and misleading at worst. One applauds the efforts in several states to make frequent revisions of master plans mandatory. Other states and districts need to follow suit, both on a large and a small scale.)

Although Table 22 presents coverage figures for the total population, it also roughly approximates conditions within the white population. It does not, however, mirror conditions for either the black or brown population. As indicated in Table 23, blacks entered the period in a slightly above-average position with 32 percent within commuting distance of a free-access college. By 1968 the figure that could have reached 59 percent, had counterforces not been in operation, had nonetheless risen to 47 percent. Most important among negative factors were selectivity, which reduced coverage 5 percent, and urbanization, which reduced it 3 percent. The Coverage Quotient was +0.56, which reflects a slightly more favorable balance between positive and negative factors than was true for the total population. Blacks in the West, however,

Table 23. Changes in percentage of black population within commuting distance of a free-access college according to accessibility factors, 1958 and 1968

Accessibility factors	Percentage within commuting distance		
	1958	1968	Net effect
New institutions	—	27	+27
Urbanization	22	19	− 3
College relocation	1	1	0
Increased costs	2	—	− 2
Increased selectivity	5	—	− 5
College closings	2	—	− 2
Total	32	47	+15

Coverage Quotient = +0.56

were affected by urbanization and college closings to such an extent that negative factors outweighed new college development, with a Coverage Quotient reading of −0.25. This coincides with the finding reported in Table 18 that a smaller proportion of Western blacks, specifically those in California, were within commuting distance of a free-access college in 1968 than in 1958.

Table 24. Changes in percentage of brown population within commuting distance of a free-access college according to accessibility factors, 1958 and 1968

Accessibility factors	Percentage within commuting distance		
	1958	1968	Net effect
New institutions	—	18	+18
Urbanization	39	29	−10
College relocation	1	0	− 1
Increased costs	1	—	− 1
Increased selectivity	6	—	− 6
College closings	1	—	− 1
Total	48	47	− 1

Coverage Quotient = −0.06

Puerto Ricans and Mexican Americans suffered quite a different fate from either whites or blacks. (Table 24.) Where in 1958 they had the best chance of living within commuting distance of a readily accessible institution, within 10 years urbanization, increased selectivity, and below-average coverage by new colleges combined to leave these groups in an unimproved state. The Coverage Quotient, in fact, was −0.06. Despite this lack of progress, their 1968 coverage was significantly above the national average.

Table 25 again demonstrates the lack of progress in the Midwest over the past decade. Its new institutions not only provided the least coverage of any region (16 percent), but the area also accounted for the second largest percentage being lost because of negative factors (14 percent). From a glance at the Midwest's Coverage Quotient, one can deduce that nearly all the growth that did occur was eroded by a combination of the other five factors.

Table 25. Changes in percentage of the population within commuting distance of a free-access college according to accessibility factors, by region, 1958 and 1968

Accessibility factors	Percentage within commuting distance							
	Northeast		Midwest		South		West	
	1958	1968	1958	1968	1958	1968	1958	1968
New institutions.	—	32	—	16	—	29	—	19
Urbanization	7	6	18	16	25	21	34	32
College relocation	0	0	2	1	1	0	1	0
Increased costs	0	—	2	—	2	—	2	—
Increased selectivity	4	—	7	—	7	—	5	—
College closings	4	—	2	—	1	—	2	—
Total.	15	38	31	33	36	50	44	51
Coverage Quotient	+0.72		+0.13		+0.48		+0.37	

The West was in a similar situation as nearly two-thirds of its modest growth was counteracted by negative factors, primarily increased selectivity. The coverage distribution for both years, however, demonstrates the long-standing commitment this region has made to its residents, in that one-third of all Westerners live within commuting distance of an institution that has been at "the same old stand" for at least a decade.

The South and Northeast have achieved nearly equal coverage with their new institutions, but they went about it in different ways. The South spread its new colleges throughout metropolitan and nonmetropolitan areas of all sizes, whereas the Northeast covered its largest groups with a relatively small number of colleges situated in metropolitan areas of at least a half million.

It may seem unusual that the South, the nation's least urbanized region, would lead all others in coverage lost through urbanization, but in fact this is the only region to have a greater proportion of its residents in each metro-politan area category in 1968 than in 1958. People have left the rural areas in large enough numbers so that for the first time in history the South has a mi-nority of its population in nonmetropolitan areas. Further evidence of the urban trend in the South is the fact that the proportion of residents living in a metro-politan area of more than a million has tripled within the decade.

Major metropolitan areas across the country were the least affected by negative factors. (Table 26.) This is not so much a cause for rejoicing as it is a recognition of the fact that 10 years ago there was comparatively little free-access higher education in these areas.

Table 26. Changes in percentage of the population within commuting distance of a free-access college according to accessibility factors, by type of community, 1958 and 1968

| | Percentage within commuting distance | | | | | |
| | Major metropolitan areas (1 million +) | | Other metropolitan areas | | Nonmetropolitan areas | |
	1958	1968	1958	1968	1958	1968
New institutions	—	22	—	30	—	23
Urbanization.	15	14	19	19	21	19
College relocation	2	1	0	0	0	0
Increased costs	0	—	3	—	2	—
Increased selectivity	2	—	9	—	8	—
College closings.	3	—	4	—	1	—
Total	22	38*	35	49	32	42
Coverage Quotient	+0.73		+0.47		+0.43	

* Detail does not add to total because of rounding.

Smaller metropolitan areas had the highest rate of coverage from new col-leges, but a great deal of the increase was offset by those institutions, in-cluding several state universities, that increased their admissions require-ments and by 10 colleges that closed. Since these areas began the decade with better than average coverage, their approximately average growth has allowed them to maintain their standing as "most accessible" among com-munities.

The problems and possibilities that confront higher education in each geo-graphic and demographic area undoubtedly vary. It is hoped this mode of analysis helps to clarify some of the components of change that have been instrumental in bringing to the people of the United States the most expansive and expensive system of free-access higher education in the world. No other nation has succeeded in creating universal access to higher education, but then again, no other nation has tried. The United States is trying; it remains to be seen whether or not she will succeed. The extent to which achievement of this condition will result in moving toward related goals, such as real enhancement of individual opportunity and significant improvement in societal affairs, also remains to be seen.

5. Summary and implications

Higher education in the United States has undergone metamorphic development in the past 25 years. The view that college attendance is essentially the privilege of the few who have demonstrated academic superiority has been largely superseded by the conviction that opportunity must be available to all who might reasonably be expected to profit from it. This latter position has been, and continues to be, the subject of varied interpretation and the object of vigorous debate, but the effects of such a philosophical shift on the higher educational enterprise have been staggering, particularly in the past decade. Between 1958 and 1968 nearly 600 new institutions were established, student enrollments more than doubled, and current expenditures more than tripled. As the seventies begin, more than half of all college-age young people are knocking on the doors of higher education and demanding admittance.

Whether this trend will lead to universal higher education (that is, college attendance by all high school graduates) is problematic. There is even widespread opinion that such a state of affairs would destroy the value of higher education as a national resource. As valid as such comments may be, they are tangential to the basic issue. The issue is not whether there should be universal attendance, but rather whether there should be universal access. The difference between the two is dramatic. Few recommend the former, many the latter. The Carnegie Commission on Higher Education, for example, has argued strongly for universal access but equally strongly against universal attendance: "We do not believe that each young person should of necessity attend college. Quite the contrary. Many do not want and will not want to attend, and it cannot be shown that all young persons will benefit sufficiently from attendance to justify their time and the expense involved. . . . We favor, on the other hand, universal *access* for those who want to enter institutions, are able to make reasonable progress after enrollment, and can benefit from attendance" (Carnegie Commission on Higher Education, 1970a).

This report has suggested that there are four categories of barriers that tend to limit access—finances, academics, motivation, and geography. Then, operating on the assumption that a large number of young people are denied educational opportunity simply because there is no low-cost, nonselective institution within commuting distance, a national study was undertaken to determine:

1. The extent to which various geographic and demographic groups did live in proximity to a free-access college in 1958,

2. The extent to which such circumstances changed between 1958 and 1968, and

3. The existence and relative importance of a number of factors instrumental in that change.

This study was made possible by the availability of data from a national demographic analysis of the accessibility of higher education as of fall 1968 conducted by Warren W. Willingham of the College Entrance Examination Board. In order to develop comparable data for 1958, Willingham's methodology was applied. This methodology basically involved three procedures: (1) the determination of those institutions that actually enrolled most high school graduates and charged tuition and fees no more than 5 percent of the median family income and that could, therefore, be defined as readily accessible (or free-access); (2) the placement of these free-access colleges on detailed maps with commuting areas ranging from 2.5 to 25 miles, depending on population density; and (3) the estimation of the various populations living within those areas. The two sets of data were also analyzed in terms of six factors — new institutions, urbanization, college relocation, increased costs, increased selectivity, and college closings — by dividing the free-access colleges into one of six groups based upon their accessibility status in both 1958 and 1968 and on whether or not they had changed locations within that period.

National findings

The principal national findings that illustrate various kinds of change with respect to the accessibility of higher education include:

1. The increase in the number of all institutions from 1,890 in 1958 to 2,596 in 1968;

2. The proportion of freshmen attending public two-year colleges doubled from 20 percent to 40 percent in 10 years;

3. The number of free-access colleges, almost all of them public, increased from 538 in 1958 to 789 in 1968;

4. Institutions that were low-cost but at least moderately selective more than doubled during the decade (146 to 356);

5. In 1958 two-year and four-year free-access institutions enrolled roughly the same number of freshmen, but by 1968 more than four times as many were enrolled in two-year rather than four-year colleges;

6. 88 state colleges and universities that were free-access in 1958 were too selective in 1968;

7. Where 30 percent of the population lived within commuting distance of a free-access college in 1958, 42 percent did in 1968;

8. Coverage increased significantly in communities of all sizes, except metropolitan areas with a population of one-half to one million and rural counties of less than 20,000;

9. Fringe areas of the 29 major metropolitan areas had the largest net increase in number of free-access institutions;

10. New institutions increased coverage of blacks and whites from about 30 percent to 55 percent of the population, but approximately half of that gain was eroded by other factors;

11. There was no increase in proportion of Puerto Ricans and Mexican Americans covered because the 18 percent gain from new institutions was counterbalanced by an equal loss through urbanization and the increased selectivity of several proximal institutions;

12. Increased selectivity among free-access colleges in 1958 was the primary negative factor and had an approximately equal impact on all groups;

13. Urbanization affected minority groups much more than it did whites.

Regional findings

Examination of changes within regions and comparison among regions also yielded consequential results. In a nutshell: through substantial development of free-access opportunities over the past 10 years the South is now roughly on a par with the West, long the acknowledged accessibility leader. The Northeast, meanwhile, has awakened to its need for accessible higher education and has grown sufficiently in this regard to surpass the Midwest on most indices of growth and 1968 status. The Midwest had virtually no increase in coverage, although it did establish a number of new free-access institutions.

Following is a listing of the more important regional findings, including the states within each region that had the largest proportion of residents within commuting distance of a free-access college in 1968 as well as those that exhibited the greatest increase in coverage between 1958 and 1968. At the end of each regional account is a brief discussion of some of the major problems that currently seem to plague that particular region.

Northeast

- The number of all institutions increased from 469 in 1958 to 647 in 1968; the number of free-access colleges expanded from 29 to 92.

- The proportion of freshmen enrolled in free-access colleges jumped from 5 percent to 22 percent but was considerably below the national average in both years.

- Few public four-year institutions were accessible in either year.

- The percentage of coverage more than doubled (15 percent to 38 percent) but was still below the national average in 1968; the increase was even greater for blacks and Puerto Ricans (30 percent and 36 percent, respectively).

- Major metropolitan areas had coverage considerably below the regional average in both years; several major central cities had no free-access college in 1958; Boston, Buffalo, and Paterson-Clifton-Passaic still had none in 1968.

- Having had so little accessible higher education, negative factors did not affect coverage greatly.

Highest 1968 coverage: Connecticut, Massachusetts

Largest 1958-1968 growth: New Hampshire, Rhode Island

Major problems: With the exception of two states, state appropriations for public higher education are penurious. In most states strengthening existing institutions and convincing the public of their legitimacy is as important a task as establishing new ones. Also, despite a large increase in coverage since 1958, more than 70 percent of the population of the seven major metropolitan areas (taken together they include more than half of all residents of the region) was beyond the range of an accessible institution in 1968. New York City, furthermore, was the only major central city to have more than one such college, and, of course, its recent move toward "open admissions" has altered its accessibility situation drastically. Political decision-makers in large metropolitan areas both in the Northeast and throughout the nation have yet to be convinced that coverage provided by a single institution is insufficient in highly congested areas.

Midwest

- There were 562 institutions in 1958 and 740 in 1968; 164 were free-access colleges in 1958, 193 in 1968.
- The proportion of freshmen enrolled in free-access institutions dropped from 37 percent to 34 percent and was below the national average in both years.
- Where two-thirds of its public four-year institutions were accessible in 1958, only one-fourth were in 1968.
- Its population coverage remained fairly stable (31 percent to 33 percent), but in doing so it dropped to last among regions.
- Apart from the Chicago and St. Louis areas, metropolitan areas of one-half million or more had very low coverage.
- Its new institutions provided opportunity to a lower percentage of the region's residents than any other region; what gain was made was almost completely washed away by negative factors, primarily increased selectivity.

Highest 1968 coverage: Illinois, Wisconsin
Largest 1958-1968 growth: Missouri, Illinois
Major problems: With respect to college accessibility the Midwest has essentially been marking time for the past 10 years. With certain notable exceptions, states have tended to shy away from strong central coordination, a posture which in not a few cases has resulted in haphazard institutional development. The Midwest has found it difficult to come to grips with the fact that their public four-year institutions, champions of egalitarianism that they once were, now shut out students on grounds of academic selectivity and, in some instances, cost. Branch campuses, of which there are a good number, have also tended to maintain similar admissions characteristics so that many students have been forced to cast about for a proximal community college. Unfortunately, in many large cities such institutions have not been available, and students, particularly impoverished students, have found themselves out of alternatives. There are signs, however, that this situation is changing. Community colleges are becoming more plentiful, and if some of the 84 moderately selective public four-year main and/or branch campuses could adjust their entrance requirements, the accessibility picture in the Midwest would brighten considerably.

South

- There were 595 colleges and universities in 1958 and 821 in 1968; at the same time free-access colleges increased from 216 to 312.

- About one-half of all freshmen attended free-access institutions in both years.

- This was the only region still to have nearly half its public four-year institutions readily accessible in 1968.

- Its overall population coverage increased from 36 percent to 50 percent.

- The coverage for communities of all sizes was at or above the national average in both years.

- Twice as many new institutions were established as in any other region.

- Although coverage from new institutions was higher than in any other region except the Northeast, urbanization and increased selectivity also affected this region more than any other.

Highest 1968 coverage: North Carolina, Mississippi

Largest 1958-1968 growth: Virginia, Florida

Major problems: Although these data show approximately equal coverage for blacks and whites, the problems of de facto segregation, and hence restricted accessibility, cannot be discounted. Also, the inadequate state appropriations present difficulties for institutions trying to effectively serve the populations within commuting distance. A third problem is the possibility that those public four-year institutions still accessible will follow the selective path of their counterparts in other regions. The trend is in that direction as 25 percent dropped out of the free-access ranks between 1958 and 1968. A fourth problem is the region's trend toward urbanization. Since it still remains the least urbanized of all regions despite this movement, policy makers may not be prepared to counteract the increased congestion of large cities with sufficient new colleges in close proximity to one another to assure adequate coverage. If they are not, the experiences in Houston and Memphis, described in Chapters 3 and 4, respectively, may be repeated in other locations throughout the region.

West

- There were 264 institutions in 1958 and 388 in 1968; nearly half in each year were free-access (129 and 192).

- Although the South had far more free-access colleges in 1968 than any other region, the West had by far the largest proportion of free-access colleges per one million population.

- More than 7 out of 10 freshmen attended a free-access institution in both years.

- Half of all public four-year colleges were readily accessible in 1958 but less than a third were accessible 10 years later.

- Its population coverage increased from 44 percent to 51 percent, with the largest growth in metropolitan areas of 250,000 to one million.

- With fringe areas of major metropolitan areas growing so rapidly, more than twice as many new institutions were established there as in the central cities; fringe areas had the highest proportion of coverage of any type of community in both 1958 and 1968.

- Central city coverage in 1968 was well below the regional average and below that of all other areas except rural counties; this represents a loss in relative position from 10 years earlier when it practically matched the regional average.

- Two-thirds of the increase in coverage brought about by new institutions was eroded by a combination of negative factors, principally increased selectivity.

- The increase in coverage of blacks was more than counteracted by various factors, primarily urbanization and college closing, so that they actually lost coverage from 52 percent to 48 percent.

Highest 1968 coverage: California, Washington

Largest 1958-1968 growth: Hawaii, Colorado

Major problems: With the constant movement of people from the major central cities to the fringe areas, pressure has been applied to establish community colleges in the latter locations. As in other regions, involvement in problems of the central cities is often politically unattractive, and the assumption seems to be made that since the population is remaining fairly stable (Los Angeles to the contrary), whatever provisions have been made in the past ought to be sufficient for the future. Unfortunately, past provisions were not adequate, populations have shifted, neighborhoods have changed, and people particularly in need of free-access higher education have in some cases moved several miles away from the nearest accessible institution. A second problem results from the fact that more than 70 percent of all freshmen begin their college careers in community colleges. What happens to those who want to transfer? Will there be room anywhere for them? The situation is already at the critical stage in many parts of California where state colleges simply do not have room, and it is bound to get both worse in that state and more pervasive throughout the region (and throughout the country, for that matter).

Concluding comments

The relationship between statewide planning and coordination and increased access to higher education is complex and does not easily submit to generalizations. Although individuals have frequently argued that increased emphasis on planning and coordination would lead to increased accessibility, available data are ambiguous. One fact is obvious; states with no master plan and no statewide coordinating board created by statute demonstrated little access growth during the 1960s (for example, Indiana and Nebraska). But on the other hand, where some states that initiated extensive planning and coordination have shown remarkable improvements in accessibility (for example, Florida and Virginia), others have not (for example, Georgia and Ohio).

There are a host of factors that have been instrumental in creating this uneven picture. They stem from demographic, educational, philosophical, and political considerations that are mixed in varying proportions from state to state. Some of these factors are listed below, and each is followed by a question or two directed to state educators and politicians concerned with increasing accessibility. The list of factors is exemplary rather than exhaustive, and the various questions are not intended to cover all possible alternatives. Nevertheless, it is hoped they bring to light some of the issues related to both accessibility and statewide planning and coordination.

1. Commitment to universal access to higher education
— Should higher education be available only to those who have distinguished themselves academically at the secondary level?
— Or, should any high school graduate or any adult be able to participate in higher education if he so chooses?
2. Models of free-access higher education
— Do data support the assumption that the primary institutional model used within your state to increase accessibility (for example, branch campuses, comprehensive community colleges, state university-controlled community colleges, technical institutes, senior colleges, and so forth) is adequate to meet state educational needs and goals?
3. Fiscal priorities
— Is the money distributed to free-access colleges sufficient to allow for adequate development both in terms of physical capacity to enroll students and in creation of relevant educational opportunities?
— Is the state and local tax structure such that low-income neighborhoods find it especially difficult to meet the postsecondary educational needs of their residents?
4. Population distribution
— Have your state's free-access colleges been located in areas where they are of maximum benefit to the students for whom they were particularly designed?
— To what extent do these colleges enroll the students for whom they were particularly designed?
— To what extent are educational opportunities readily accessible to residents in communities of varying sizes?
5. Purposes and structure of statewide planning and coordinating agencies
— Is there general understanding and acceptance of the raison d'être of your statewide agency?
— To what extent do agency actions or recommendations receive support and carry weight within the educational and political communities?
6. Clarity of role definition for statewide planning and coordinating agencies
— Is there educational, political, and staff consensus on the particular roles

and functions the agency should carry out?

— Are these generally accepted functions likely to lead to increased access to college?

7. Longevity of statewide planning and coordinating agencies

— Is the agency so new that its effect upon accessibility has not had time to be measured?

— What efforts are being made to evaluate the activities and the effectiveness of the agency?

— Is the effectiveness of your agency in increasing accessibility impaired because it continues to operate under a mandate that restricts its powers or activities in this area?

To repeat, there are many more questions that need asking, and behind the answer to each lies another series of questions that also need answers. Only at this point can one begin to gain an understanding of the reasons certain states have increased access to college greatly in the past decade while others have lagged behind. This statement should not be construed as a suggestion for endless undue contemplation but rather as a call for thoughtful evaluation followed by whatever action is deemed appropriate.

Earlier in this chapter a legitimate question was sidestepped — should each state actually strive toward the goal of placing a free-access college within reach of nearly all its residents? Allusion was made to advocacy of universal access, as well as opposition to universal attendance. Can one, however, really exist without the other? Or, is it possible that attendance would be even more obligatory as opportunities[1] expanded? Would not the enlarged pool of college attendees entering the labor market force those who might not otherwise desire to enter college feel compelled to do so out of sheer economic pressure?

Given the present structure of our society and the exalted position of a degree-holder in the marketplace, such an outcome certainly must be considered a possibility. It is conceivable, however, that alternate means of postsecondary learning and growth will become viable for large groups of young people. For example, educational programs sponsored by industry, labor unions, the armed forces, the federal government, museums, correspondence schools, and television stations have grown substantially in the past decade. And this movement has been given new impetus recently by numerous proposals for external degree institutions (Carnegie Commission, 1971; *Chronicle of Higher Education,* 1971; Pifer, 1970) and the development of a College Board-sponsored Commission on Nontraditional Study, chaired by Samuel Gould, former Chancellor of the State University of New York.

Although large numbers of young people (and adults, as well) may participate in some form of postsecondary education, universal attendance as it is

---

1. In this study the terms "opportunity" and "accessibility" have been used interchangeably on several occasions. It should be pointed out, however, that genuine opportunity consists of far more than just living near a college. Various questions regarding relevance come into play, and the interested reader is encouraged to note the excellent discussion of this complex topic in Chapter 7 of Willingham's study as well as the brief treatment given in my monograph, "Barriers to Universal Higher Education."

discussed and feared by many today is not a necessary appendage to universal access. What the universal presence of accessible institutions would specifically accomplish is the reduction of some of those artificial barriers that presently tend to keep certain kinds of young people from obtaining higher education. Too often today the basis for sorting those that "get" from those that "get not" is an individual's supply of funds, familiarity with the academic treadmill, degree of motivation, proximity to an institution, or any combination of the four, whereas it would seem more reasonable and infinitely more just to base selection on potential to succeed.

The key to the success of an educational system based on potential lies in diversity of institutions; in perceptive, intelligent counseling; and in creative admissions personnel. It would not serve either society or students well if all institutions attempted to perform the same functions and serve the same clientele. (This is, of course, one of today's problems.) Each college and university must chart its own course, and, more important, follow it. Some institutions ought to provide programs in which only the most capable are likely to succeed. To paraphrase Gardner, not everyone has the right to graduate from MIT, any more than everyone has the right to run a four-minute mile. Other colleges ought to provide a structure and programs that will serve the student in need of a small, congenial atmosphere. Still others ought to be oriented toward continuing education. A large number ought to offer comprehensive programs in a supportive environment close to home for the substantial number of students who choose to test their wings there. Some of these students will fly well and go on to other programs and other institutions; some will not get off the ground. Both groups need expert guidance. So, too, do those high school students who may wish to choose an alternative to higher education. Often the forgotten ones, these students need to have counseling and guidance services available to them not only during the high school years, but also for several years beyond.

On the basis of past performances and the magnitude of the task that lies ahead, one cannot be sanguine that the day of universal access to higher education will dawn soon. While new institutions will continue to be constructed, restricted funds may slow their rate of growth while ever-increasing urbanization retards their effect. The pronounced tendency to construct community colleges outside central cities will have to be at least partially overcome. Selectivity is likely to continue to be a major factor as the majority of public four-year colleges readily accessible in 1968 follow the pattern set in the past decade by similar institutions. The possibility exists, of course, that this emphasis on selectivity could decrease if pressure for "open admissions" increases and if enrollment growth tapers off within the next 10 years as projected. Whatever the outcome of these developments, one must hope that two-year colleges will not travel the route toward inaccessibility that four-year institutions in large measure have trod.

Appendix

Percentage of populations within commuting distance of free-access colleges in each metropolitan area of one million or more, 1958 and 1968

Metropolitan area	Population in millions		Percent within commuting distance		
	1958	1968	1958	1968	Change
Anaheim	.22	.70	80	89	+ 9
City	.06	.29	94	100	+ 6
Fringe	.15	.42	74	81	+ 7
Atlanta	.67	1.02	62	25	−37
City	.33	.49	100	13	−87
Fringe	.34	.53	25	34	+ 9
Baltimore	1.34	1.73	39	37	− 2
City	.95	.94	40	37	− 3
Fringe	.39	.79	36	38	+ 2
Boston	2.37	2.60	2	21	+19
City	.80	.70	0	15	+15
Fringe	1.57	1.90	3	35	+32
Buffalo	1.09	1.31	44	32	−12
City	.58	.53	82	17	−65
Fringe	.51	.77	0	42	+42
Chicago	5.50	6.22	52	58	+ 6
City	3.62	3.56	63	67	+ 4
Fringe	1.87	2.67	31	46	+15
Cincinnati	.90	1.27	40	5	−35
City	.50	.50	70	0	−70
Fringe	.40	.77	3	10	+ 7
Cleveland	1.47	1.91	11	24	+13
City	.91	.88	18	30	+12
Fringe	.55	1.03	0	19	+19
Dallas	.61	1.12	5	14	+ 9
City	.43	.68	0	18	+18
Fringe	.18	.44	17	7	−10
Denver	.56	.93	0	35	+35
City	.42	.49	0	47	+47
Fringe	.15	.44	0	22	+22
Detroit	3.02	3.76	21	29	+ 8
City	1.85	1.67	17	16	− 1
Fringe	1.17	2.09	27	39	+12
Houston	.81	1.42	80	18	−62
City	.60	.94	95	13	−82
Fringe	.21	.48	38	28	−10
Kansas City	.81	1.09	33	21	−12
City	.59	.60	44	38	− 6
Fringe	.23	.50	3	0	− 3
Los Angeles	4.15	6.04	55	58	+ 5
City	1.97	2.82	41	44	+ 3
Fringe	2.18	3.22	67	71	+ 4

Percentage of populations within commuting distance of free-access colleges in each metropolitan area of one million or more, 1958 and 1968 (continued)

Metropolitan area	Population in millions		Percent within commuting distance		
	1958	1968	1958	1968	Change
Miami	.50	.94	0	50	+50
City	.25	.29	0	94	+94
Fringe	.25	.64	0	31	+31
Milwaukee	.87	1.28	90	23	−67
City	.64	.74	100	37	−63
Fringe	.23	.54	63	2	−61
Minneapolis	1.12	1.48	0	25	+25
City	.83	.80	0	26	+26
Fringe	.28	.69	0	24	+24
Newark	1.47	1.69	10	33	+23
City	.44	.41	35	77	+42
Fringe	1.03	1.28	0	19	+19
New Orleans	.69	.91	0	32	+32
City	.57	.63	0	42	+42
Fringe	.12	.28	0	10	+10
New York	10.57	10.69	7	29	+22
City	7.89	7.78	0	29	+29
Fringe	2.68	2.91	28	29	+ 1
Paterson	.88	1.19	37	0	−37
City	.26	.28	66	0	−66
Fringe	.61	.91	25	0	−25
Philadelphia	3.67	4.34	2	29	+27
City	2.07	2.00	0	29	+29
Fringe	1.60	2.34	5	29	+24
Pittsburgh	2.21	2.41	1	28	+27
City	.68	.60	0	35	+35
Fringe	1.54	1.80	1	26	+25
St. Louis	1.68	2.10	3	46	+43
City	.86	.75	0	71	+71
Fringe	.82	1.35	5	32	+27
San Bernardino	.45	.81	38	45	+ 7
City	.13	.22	100	77	−23
Fringe	.32	.59	12	32	+20
San Diego	.56	1.03	40	39	− 1
City	.33	.57	50	31	−19
Fringe	.22	.46	25	49	+24
San Francisco	2.24	2.65	45	55	+10
City	1.16	1.11	47	37	−10
Fringe	1.08	1.54	44	68	+24
Seattle	.73	1.11	55	45	−10
City	.47	.56	86	32	−54
Fringe	.27	.55	0	57	+57

Percentage of populations within commuting distance of free-access colleges in each metropolitan area of one million or more, 1958 and 1968 (continued)

Metropolitan area	Population in millions		Percent within commuting distance		
	1958	1968	1958	1968	Change
Washington, D. C.	1.46	2.08	30	71	+41
City	.80	.76	34	82	+48
Fringe	.66	1.31	24	65	+41
SMSA* Total	52.61	65.81	25	37	+12
City	30.24	32.58	27	37	+10
Fringe	22.37	33.23	23	37	+14

*Standard Metropolitan Statistical Areas

Bibliography

Adams, Walter, "Caste and Class, Relative Deprivation, and Higher Education." New York: Bureau of Applied Social Research, Columbia University, 1968, 47 pp. Mimeographed.

American Council on Education, "Community College Bill Introduced by 28 Senators." *Higher Education and National Affairs,* Vol. 38, No. 6, 1969, p. 11.

Astin, Alexander W., "Racial Considerations in College Admissions." Washington, D.C.: American Council on Education, 1969, 28 pp. Mimeographed.

Astin, Alexander W.; Panos, Robert J.; and Creager, John A., "National Norms for Entering College Freshmen—Fall 1966." *American Council on Education Research Reports,* Vol. 2, No. 1, 1967, pp. 22–23.

Axelrod, Joseph, and others, *Search for Relevance.* San Francisco: Jossey-Bass, Inc., Publishers, 1969, 244 pp.

Baird, Leonard L.; Richards, James M. Jr.; and Shevel, Linda R., "A Description of Graduates of Two-Year Colleges." *American College Testing Research Report,* No. 28, January 1969, pp. 1–25

Bashaw, Wilbur L., "The Effect of Community Junior Colleges on the Proportion of the Local Population Who Seek Higher Education." *Journal of Educational Research,* Vol. 58, No. 7, March 1965, pp. 327–329.

Berdahl, Robert O., *Statewide Coordination of Higher Education.* Washington, D. C.: American Council on Education, 1971, 285 pp.

Billings, Thomas A., "Upward Bound Works." *Educational Opportunity Forum,* Winter 1968, pp. 1–2.

Blocker, Clyde E.; Plummer, Robert H.; and Richardson, Richard C. Jr., *The Two-Year College: A Social Synthesis.* Englewood Cliffs, N.J.: Prentice-Hall, Inc., 1965, 298 pp.

Bowen, Howard R., "Who Pays the Higher Education Bill?" In Southern Regional Education Board, *Proceedings: A Symposium on Financing Higher Education.* Atlanta, Ga.: Southern Regional Education Board, 1969, pp. 3–14.

Bowles, Frank, "Access to Education—A Global View." *College Board Review,* Fall 1962, No. 48, pp. 7–15.

Carnegie Commission on Higher Education, *A Chance to Learn.* New York: McGraw-Hill Book Company, 1970a, 31 pp.

Carnegie Commission on Higher Education, *Less Time, More Options: Education Beyond the High School.* New York: McGraw-Hill Book Company, 1971, 45 pp.

Carnegie Commission on Higher Education, *The Open-Door Colleges: Policies for Community Colleges.* New York: McGraw-Hill Book Company, 1970b, 74 pp.

Carnegie Commission on Higher Education, *Quality and Equality: New Levels of Federal Responsibility for Higher Education.* New York: McGraw-Hill Book Company, 1968, 54 pp.

Chronicle of Higher Education, "A National 'Open University' Is on Its Way, Educators Told." Vol. 5, No. 24, March 22, 1971, p. 1.

Chronicle of Higher Education, "Bowdoin Will Stop Requiring Tests of Applicants." Vol. 4, No. 17, February 2, 1970a, p. 1.

Chronicle of Higher Education, "Negro Enrollments this Year on the Nation's Campuses." Vol. 3, No. 16, April 21, 1969a, pp. 3–4.

Chronicle of Higher Education, "Nixon Administration Seen Giving High Priority to Two-Year Colleges," Vol. 3, No. 17, May 5, 1969b, p. 1.

Chronicle of Higher Education, "Sixty-Nine Percent of Opportunity Grants Go to Low-Income Students." Vol. 4, No. 14, Janauary 12, 1970b, p. 7.

Clark, Burton R., "The 'Cooling Out' Function in Higher Education." *American Journal of Sociology,* Vol. 65, No. 6, May 1960, pp. 569–576.

Clark, Kenneth B., *Dark Ghetto.* New York: Harper & Row, Publishers, 1965, 251 pp.

Coleman, James S., "The Concept of Equality of Educational Opportunity." *Harvard Educational Review,* Vol. 38, No. 1, 1968, pp. 7–22.

Coleman, James S., and others, *Equality of Educational Opportunity.* Washington, D.C.: U.S. Department of Health, Education, and Welfare, Office of Education, 1966, 737 pp.

Cosand, J. P., "Philosophy of Community Junior Colleges." *School and Community,* Vol. 53, November 1966, pp. 35–36, 87–91.

Crawford, N. C. Jr., "Effects of Offers of Financial Assistance on the College Going Decisions of Talented Students with Limited Financial Means." *National Merit Scholarship Corporation Research Reports,* Vol. 3, No. 5, 1967, pp. 1–21.

Daughtry, Alex A., and Hawk, Richard C., "A Report on the Post-Graduation Activities of the 1957 High School Graduates." *Kansas State Teachers College Bulletin of Information,* Vol. 38, No. 11, September 1958, 45 pp.

Dennis, Lawrence E., "Equalizing Educational Opportunity for the Disadvantaged," in Mayhew, Lewis B., ed., *Higher Education in the Revolutionary Decades.* Berkeley, Calif.: McCutchan Publishing Corp., 1967, pp. 297–304.

Dressel, Paul, *College and University Curriculum.* Berkeley, Calif.: McCutchan Publishing Corp., 1968, 232 pp.

Editorial Projects for Education, "Community College Bill Offered." *Chronicle of Higher Education,* Vol. 3, No. 12, February 24, 1969, p. 5.

Educational Associates, Inc., *A Report on Upward Bound to the Office of Economic Opportunity.* Washington, D.C.: Educational Associates, Inc., 1969, 35 pp.

Educational Policies Commission, *American Education and the Search for Equal Opportunity.* Washington, D.C.: National Education Association, 1965, 37 pp.

Educational Policies Commission, *Universal Opportunities for Education Beyond the High School.* Washington, D.C.: National Education Association, 1964, 36 pp.

Egerton, John, "Almost All-White." *Southern Education Report,* Vol. 4, No. 9, May 1969, pp. 2–17.

Ferrin, Richard I., *Barriers to Universal Higher Education.* Access Research Office, College Entrance Examination Board, 1970, 62 pp. Unpublished.

Ferrin, Richard I., *Developmental Programs in Midwestern Community Colleges.* New York: College Entrance Examination Board, 1971, 50 pp.

Ferrin, Richard I., *Student Budgets and Aid Awarded in Southwestern Colleges.* New York: College Entrance Examination Board, 1971, 40 pp.

Ferrin, Richard I., and Willingham, Warren W., *Practices of Southern Institutions in Recognizing College-Level Achievement.* New York: College Entrance Examination Board, 1970, 42 pp.

Florida State Department of Education, *The Community Junior College in Florida's Future.* Tallahassee: Florida State Department of Education, 1957, 71 pp.

Florida State Department of Education, *Florida Community Junior Colleges: Highlights of a Decade.* Tallahassee: Florida State Department of Education, 1967, 36 pp.

Froomkin, Joseph, *Students and Buildings: An Analysis of Selected Federal Programs for Higher Education.* Washington, D.C.: U.S. Office of Education, 1968, 72 pp.

Gleazer, Edmund J. Jr., "Junior College Explosion." *American Education,* Vol. 5, No. 1, 1969, pp. 12–13.

Hazen Foundation, *The Student in Higher Education.* New Haven, Conn.: The Hazen Foundation, 1968, 66 pp.

Healy, Timothy S., "Will Everyone Destroy the University?" *Saturday Review,* December 20, 1969, p. 68.

Hechinger, Fred M., "For Equality of Opportunity." *The New York Times,* December 15, 1968, p. 9E.

Hess, R. D.; Shipman, V.; and Jackson, D., "Some New Dimensions in Providing Equal Educational Opportunity." *Journal of Negro Education,* Vol. 34, 1965, pp. 220–231.

Hollingshead, August B., *Elmtown's Youth.* New York: John Wiley & Sons, Inc., 1949, 480 pp.

Hood, Albert B., *What Type of College for What Type of Student?* Minneapolis: University of Minnesota Press, 1968, 84 pp.

Jacobson, Robert L., "Clark Kerr Changes View, Backs Public-College Tuition." *Chronicle of Higher Education,* Vol. 4, No. 14, Janaury 12, 1970, p. 4.

Jacobson, Robert L., "Education Gain by Poor Called 'Revolutionary.'" *Chronicle of Higher Education,* Vol. 3, No. 13, March 10, 1969a, p. 1.

Jacobson, Robert L., "Finch Promises Junior College 'Cover' Plan." *Chronicle of Higher Education,* Vol. 4, No. 3, October 13, 1969b, p. 4.

Jaffe, A. J.; Adams, Walter; and Meyers, S. G., *Negro Higher Education in the 1960s.* New York: Frederick A. Praeger, Inc., 1968, 290 pp.

Jencks, Christopher, "Social Stratification and Higher Education." *Harvard Educational Review,* Vol. 38, No. 2, Spring 1968a, pp. 277–316.

Jencks, Christopher, and Riesman, David, *The Academic Revolution.* Garden City, N.Y.: Doubleday & Company, Inc., 1968b, 580 pp.

Kendrick, S. A., *Extending Educational Opportunity — Problems of Recruitment and Admissions, High Risk Students, Cultural Deprivation, etc.* Washington, D.C.: Association of American Colleges, 1969, 3 pp.

Kerr, Clark, *Higher Education in the Troubled City.* Berkeley, Calif.: Carnegie Commission on the Future of Higher Education, 1968a, 20 pp.

Kerr, Clark, *The Urban-Grant University: A Model for the Future.* New York: City University of New York, 1968b, 14 pp.

Knoell, Dorothy M., "Are Our Colleges Really Accessible to the Poor?" *Junior College Journal,* Vol. 39, No. 2, October 1968, pp. 9–11.

Knoell, Dorothy M., *Toward Educational Opportunity for All.* Albany: State University of New York, 1966, 220 pp.

Koos, Leonard V., "How to Democratize the Junior College Level." *School Review,* May 1944a, pp. 271–284.

Koos, Leonard V., "Local versus Regional Junior Colleges." *School Review,* November 1944b, p. 257.

Lecht, Leonard A., *Goals, Priorities, and Dollars.* New York: The Free Press, 1966, 365 pp.

Martin, Warren B., *Alternative to Irrevelance.* Nashville, Tenn.: Abingdon Press, 1968, 160 pp.

Martyn, Kenneth, *California Higher Education and Disadvantaged: A Status Report.* Sacramento, Calif.: Coordinating Council for Higher Education, March 1968, 77 pp.

Martyn, Kenneth, *Increasing Opportunities in Higher Education for Disadvantaged Students.* Sacramento, Calif.: Coordinating Council for Higher Education, 1966, 75 pp.

Mayhew, Lewis B., *Contemporary College Students and the Curriculum.* Atlanta: Southern Regional Education Board, 1969a, 86 pp.

Mayhew, Lewis B., *Higher Education in the Revolutionary Decades.* Berkeley, Calif.: McCutchan Publishing Corp., 1967, 466 pp.

Mayhew, Lewis B., *Long Range Planning for Higher Education.* Washington, D.C.: Academy for Educational Development, 1969b, 221 pp.

Medsker, Leland L., and Trent, James W., *The Influence of Different Types of Public Institutions on College Entrance from Varying Socio-economic and Ability Levels.* Berkeley, Calif.: Center for Research and Development in Higher Education, 1965, 110 pp.

Moore, William Jr., *Against the Odds.* San Francisco: Jossey-Bass, Inc., Publishers, 1970, 244 pp.

Morse, John F., "The Federal Role in Education: One View," in Southern Regional Education Board, *Proceedings: A Symposium on Financing Higher Education*. Atlanta: Southern Regional Education Board, 1969, pp. 38–44.

National Advisory Commission on Civil Disorders, *Report of the National Advisory Commission on Civil Disorders*. New York: Bantam Books, Inc., 1968, 425 pp.

National Association of State Universities and Land-Grant Colleges, and American Association of State Colleges and Universities, *Recommendations for National Action Affecting Higher Education: A Joint Statement*. Washington, D.C.: National Association of State Universities and Land-Grant Colleges, and American Association of State Colleges and Universities, February 1969, 38 pp.

O'Connell, Thomas E., *Community Colleges: A President's View*. Urbana, Ill.: University of Illinois Press, 1968, 172 pp.

O'Hara, William T., ed., *John F. Kennedy on Education*. New York: Teachers College Press, 1966, 305 pp.

Ohio Board of Regents, *Ohio's New Look in Higher Education*. Columbus, Ohio: Ohio Board of Regents, 1968, 15 pp.

Palola, Ernest G.; Lehmann, Timothy; and Blischke, William R., *Higher Education by Design: The Sociology of Planning*. Berkeley, Calif.: Center for Research and Development in Higher Education, 1970, 627 pp.

Parsons, Talcott, and Clark, Kenneth B., eds., *The Negro American*. Boston, Mass.: Houghton Mifflin Company, 1965, 781 pp.

Perrella, Vera C., "Employment of High School Graduates and Dropouts." *Monthly Labor Review,* Vol. 92, No. 6, June 1969, pp. 36–43.

Pifer, Alan, "Is It Time for an External Degree?" *College Board Review,* Winter 1970–71, No. 78, pp. 5–10.

President's Commission on Higher Education, *Higher Education for American Democracy,* Vol. 1. Washington, D.C.: U.S. Government Printing Office, 1947, 103 pp.

Roueche, J. E., *Salvage, Redirection or Custody?* Washington, D.C.: American Association of Junior Colleges, 1968, 67 pp.

Rudolph, Frederick, *The American College and University: A History*. New York: Vintage Books, 1962, 516 pp.

Sanders, Edward, and Palmer, Hans, *The Financial Barrier to Higher Education in California*. Claremont, Calif.: Pomona College, 1965, 295 pp.

Schoenfeldt, Lyle F., "Education After High School." *Sociology of Education,* Vol. 41, No. 4, 1968, pp. 350–369.

Selk, Eleanore, "Putting Muscle Behind the Reach." *Junior College Journal,* Vol. 40, No. 1, September 1969, pp. 20–22.

Sewell, William H., and Shah, Vimal P., "Social Class, Parental Encouragement, and Educational Aspirations." *American Journal of Sociology,* Vol. 73, March 1968, pp. 559–572.

Smith, G. K., ed., *Stress and Campus Response*. San Francisco: Jossey-Bass, Inc., Publishers, 1968, 297 pp.

State Junior College Advisory Board of Florida, *Five Years of Progress: Florida's Community Junior Colleges . . . Their Contributions and Their Future*. Tallahassee: State Department of Education, 1963, 47 pp.

Thornton, J. W. Jr., *The Community Junior College,* 2nd ed. New York: John Wiley & Sons, Inc., 1966, 300 pp.

Thresher, B. Alden, *College Admissions and the Public Interest*. New York: College Entrance Examination Board, 1966, 93 pp.

Trent, James W., and Medsker, Leland L., *Beyond High School*. San Francisco: Jossey-Bass, Inc., Publishers, 1968, 333 pp.

Trow, Martin, "Elite and Popular Functions in American Higher Education, in Niblett, W. R., ed., *Higher Education: Demand and Response*. San Francisco: Jossey-Bass, Inc., Publishers, 1970, pp. 181–201.

U. S. Bureau of the Census, "Income in 1968 of Families and Persons in the United States." *Current Population Reports* Series P–60, No. 66, pp. 25–26. Washington, D.C.: U. S. Department of Commerce, 1969a.

U. S. Bureau of the Census and Bureau of Labor Statistics, "The Social and Economic Status of Negroes in the United States, 1969." Bureau of Labor Statistics Report No. 375, *Current Population Reports*, Series P–23, No. 29, 1969b, 96 pp. Washington, D.C.: U. S. Department of Commerce.

U. S. Department of Commerce, *We the Mexican Americans*. Washington, D.C.: U. S. Department of Commerce, 1970, 17 pp.

U. S. Department of Commerce, Bureau of the Census, "Annual Report on the Labor Force, 1958." *Current Population Reports*, Series P–50, No. 89, June 1959, 61 pp.

U. S. Department of Labor, Bureau of Labor Statistics, *Handbook of Labor Statistics 1968*. Washington, D.C.: U. S. Government Printing Office, 1968, 350 pp.

U. S. National Commission on Technology, Automation, and Economic Progress, *Technology and the American Economy*, Vol. 1. *Outlook for Technological Change and Employment*. Washington, D.C.: U. S. Government Printing Office, 1966, 373 pp.

U. S. Office of Education, *Biennial Survey of Education in the United States, 1956–1958*. Washington, D.C.: U. S. Government Printing Office, 1962, 120 pp.

U. S. Office of Education, *Education Directory, 1958–1959*, Part 3. Washington, D.C.: U. S. Government Printing Office, 1958, 184 pp.

U. S. Office of Education, *Education Directory, 1968–1969*, Part 3. Washington, D.C.: U. S. Government Printing Office, 1968b, 140 pp.

U. S. Office of Education, *Opening Fall Enrollment*. Washington, D.C.: U. S. Government Printing Office, 1959, 33 pp.

U. S. Office of Education, *Opening Fall Enrollment in Higher Education, 1968*. Washington, D.C.: U. S. Government Printing Office, 1969b, 133 pp.

U. S. Office of Education, *Projections of Educational Statistics to 1975–1976*. Washington, D.C.: U. S. Government Printing Office, 1966a, 113 pp.

U. S. Office of Education, *Projections of Educational Statistics to 1977–1978*. Washington, D.C.: U. S. Government Printing Office, 1966b, 122 pp.

Wattenbarger, J. L., *A State Plan for Public Junior Colleges with Special Reference to Florida*. Gainesville, Fla.: University of Florida, 1953, 83 pp.

Wiggins, Sam P., Higher Education in the South. Berkeley, Calif.: McCutchan Publishing Corp., 1966, 358 pp.

Willingham, Warren W., *Free-Access Higher Education*. New York: College Entrance Examination Board, 1970, 240 pp.

Willingham, Warren W., *The Importance of Relevance in Expanding Post-Secondary Education*. New York: College Entrance Examination Board, 1969, 55 pp.

Willingham, Warren W., and Findikyan, Nurhan, *Patterns of Admission for Transfer Students*. New York: College Entrance Examination Board, 1969, 47 pp.

Willis, Benjamin C., *Higher Education. Part 1: The Chicago Teachers Colleges; Part 2: The Chicago City Junior College*. Study Report No. 10, 1964 Series, Chicago Public Schools, August 1964, 66 pp.

Willis, Benjamin C., *The Second Report on the Chicago City Junior College to the Chicago Board of Education.* Chicago Public Schools, July 23, 1958, 23 pp.

Wolfle, Dael. *America's Resources of Specialized Talent.* New York: Harper & Row, Publishers, 1954, 332 pp.

Yarrington, Roger, ed., *Junior Colleges: 50 States/50 Years.* Washington, D.C.: American Association of Junior Colleges, 1969, 297 pp.

DATE DUE

MAR 6 '73			
DEC 1 8 2009			